SMALL-SCALE TEXTILES

SPINNING

SMALL-SCALE TEXTILES

SPINNING

A Handbook

John Foulds

Intermediate Technology Publications 1988

Practical Action Publishing Ltd
27a Albert Street, Rugby, CV21 2SG, Warwickshire, UK
www.practicalactionpublishing.org

© Intermediate Technology Publications, 1988

First published 1988\Digitised 2013

ISBN 10: 1 85339 035 6
ISBN 13: 9781853390357
ISBN Library Ebook: 9781780443454
Book DOI: http://dx.doi.org/10.3362/9781780443454

All rights reserved. No part of this publication may be reprinted or reproduced or utilized in any form or by any electronic, mechanical, or other means, now known or hereafter invented, including photocopying and recording, or in any information storage or retrieval system, without the written permission of the publishers.

A catalogue record for this book is available from the British Library.

The authors, contributors and/or editors have asserted their rights under the Copyright Designs and Patents Act 1988 to be identified as authors of their respective contributions.

Since 1974, Practical Action Publishing has published and disseminated books and information in support of international development work throughout the world. Practical Action Publishing is a trading name of Practical Action Publishing Ltd (Company Reg. No. 1159018), the wholly owned publishing company of Practical Action. Practical Action Publishing trades only in support of its parent charity objectives and any profits are covenanted back to Practical Action (Charity Reg. No. 247257, Group VAT Registration No. 880 9924 76).

CONTENTS

	Page
Acknowledgements	vi
Foreword	vii
Preface	viii
Chapter 1 Introduction to spinning	1
Chapter 2 The basic principles and the process of spinning	3
Chapter 3 Simple methods of testing the quality of spun yarn	23
Chapter 4 Specification of small-scale spinning machines	30
Chapter 5 Planning for production	34
Chapter 6 Equipment suppliers	38
Chapter 7 Sources of further information	42
Appendix 1 Comparison of Tex with other count systems	45
Appendix 2 Nomogram for twist factor (Tex and Yorkshire Skein Wool)	46
Appendix 3 Nomogram for twist factor (Tex and English Cotton)	47

ACKNOWLEDGEMENTS

Even a small handbook such as this is not compiled without the help of many people. There is not room to mention them all, but we would particularly like to thank Nagin Salaria, Madan Saluja, and B.V. Iyer for much useful advice and discussion. Thanks also to Tom Halstead (Department of Textile Industries, Huddersfield Polytechnic) who read the text and made many helpful suggestions.

John Foulds

Illustrations and diagrams by Linda Combi, Roger Croston, Peter Dobson and Mike Calvert.

FOREWORD

This handbook is one of a series dealing with the whole of textile production, from raw materials to finished products. Each handbook sets out to give some of the options available to existing or potential producers, where their aims could be to create employment or sustain existing small-scale textile production with the aim of generating income for the rural poor in developing countries. Needless to say, this slim volume does not pretend to be comprehensive. It is intended as an introduction to the topic which will stimulate further enquiry. Although each handbook is complete in itself and provides useful reference material on each specific area of production, the series, taken as a whole, does reveal the breadth of technology required to equip a small-scale textile industry. While being primarily technical, the series also covers the socio-economic, managerial and marketing issues relevant to textile production in the rural areas of developing countries.

The author of this handbook has harnessed his own particular expertise and experience to produce a distillation of his technical knowledge applied to the developing world. While no single package of technology can be appropriate to all situations, he has produced a simple but logical progression covering all aspects of small-scale textile production.

Production of this series of books has been sponsored by the Intermediate Technology Development Group (ITDG), as part of its efforts to help co-ordinate the most appropriate solution to particular development needs. This series forms part of the cycle of identifying the need, recognizing the problems, and developing strategies to alleviate the crisis of un- and underemployment in the Third World.

ITDG also offers consultancy services for feasibility studies, project design and implementation, together with the identification and transfer of technology. For further information write to ITDG. We will be pleased to help.

Martin Hardingham,
Textiles Programme Manager,
ITDG, Rugby, UK

April 1988

PREFACE

Almost all textile fabrics, whether knitted or woven, are made from yarns or thread, and over half the yarns produced in the world are made by twisting short fibres together. The process of yarn making or spinning, has been used for thousands of years. The Egyptians used it for flax spinning at least 7,000 years ago and similar processes have been used to spin cotton in India, hemp in China and wool in Babylon and Assyria.

Today, yarns are spun on modern machinery all over the world, either alone or mixed with short man-made fibres. The range of machinery and methods used is very large. However, in some parts of the world, spinning fibres into yarns has always depended on the needs of the people producing the fabric and the fibres which are readily available for spinning. In the poor, largely rural areas of the developing world, there is still a need for cloth which can be made into cheap, durable and practical garments. In more affluent societies, the perceived 'need' is that fabrics should have variety, attractive appearance, or special properties using additional fibres. Manufacturing methods and finishes have been developed to meet these needs. The scale of modern textile production is such that mass-produced fabrics are available all over the world at a cost which is sometimes cheaper than any small community can produce its own hand-made fabrics. Paradoxically, this has created markets for hand-made textiles in affluent countries where they are perceived to have properties which cannot be reproduced by modern machinery.

However, rural communities can benefit more directly from the production of fabrics made by simple hand processes, provided the economic balance between raw material availability, production costs and suitable markets can be met. Quite often the benefits obtained are an adjunct to other activities, such as small-scale farming. Textile production is then undertaken to increase very low earnings.

This handbook is concerned with spinning as part of small-scale textile production and is aimed at small, rural communities and the development organizations or individual field workers involved with them. Quite often the need is for some basic information or understanding, either to start a new spinning activity or to improve an existing one. This handbook is obviously not intended to be a textbook on spinning, but should allow any interested user to know a little about the principles and processes involved and to find out where further help or knowledge is available.

John Foulds

1. INTRODUCTION TO SPINNING

This handbook is limited to the consideration of spinning on a small scale, that is to the processes which can be undertaken by hand or by use of small, power-driven equipment. The processes described are also limited to spinning natural and man-made fibres in staple form, that is in short lengths, unlike fibres in continuous filament form which lie outside the scope of this handbook.

General considerations in spinning staple fibres

All fibres have a wide range of properties which, to some extent, affect the methods used to spin them into yarns. In general, natural fibres, such as wool, cotton and flax, contain many impurities which must be removed or separated from the fibres before they can be spun, whereas man-made fibres can be spun immediately, once they have been cut or broken into a suitable staple length. Silk is a continuous filament fibre but it can also be spun as a staple fibre like wool or cotton, usually in the form of silk waste. The staple length of fibres varies. Some cotton fibres may be less than half an inch long, wool fibres may be from two to ten inches long and flax fibre bundles may be up to thirty-six inches long.

Certain fibres, such as cotton, are relatively straight wheareas others may be very crimped like some types of wool. Some may need special treatment to separate out the individual fibres: flax, jute and hemp are examples. Fibres can be strong or weak, rigid or elastic, smooth or rough.

These different properties have influenced in many ways the methods which are used to spin them. Quite often the machinery used to spin one fibre may look different from that used for another. However, the fundamental principles of making yarns from staple fibres are the same for all.

Once they are prepared for spinning, all fibres can be spun into yarns by simple hand methods using the same equipment. As soon as there is a need for greater productivity, or control of spinning, then the differences in the raw materials make the use of more complex machinery necessary to allow for the particular characteristics of each fibre.

Basic principles

The following processes are used to convert a mass of staple fibres into a yarn to meet required specifications of thickness, evenness, twist and composition:

1. Opening, cleaning, mixing and carding fibres.

2. Making the opened mass of fibres into a rope form in which all the fibres are more or less parallel with a required thickness or weight per unit length. In this form the rope of fibres is called a sliver or roving.

3. Drafting the roving of fibres (reducing the weight per unit length) by extending and drawing the fibres over each other until a desired thickness is achieved and then inserting twist to form a yarn.

4. Winding the yarn onto a bobbin or other type of package.

All these operations* must be carried out so that the final yarn is made to the desired specifications and is sufficiently even and strong for its purpose. Normally the yarn must also be made as economically as possible.

* 1 and 2 are processes described in the Handbook on pre-spinning processes. 3 and 4 are spinning operations and form the subject of this Handbook.

Drafting and twisting

These two operations form the basic actions of yarn production from staple fibres. They have been used for thousands of years to make yarns using simple drop spindles or spinning wheels, and the basic mechanism of yarn formation has not changed. Fibres which have been made into a sliver, which is a rope of fibres without any twist, either by hand or by machine carding, are still unevenly arranged, although many fibres will lie more or less parallel. In this form there is some cohesion between fibres so that the sliver can be handled without breaking. Because of the thickness of the sliver it must be reduced, often in stages, to form a roving from which a yarn can be spun. During the reduction in thickness the sliver is drafted, i.e. drawn finer by extending the sliver and allowing fibres to be drawn apart so that the sliver becomes thinner. As the fibres become more parallel during the drawing action, the cohesion between them becomes less and eventually the sliver or roving becomes too weak to handle. To increase the strength of the roving it is therefore necessary to increase the friction between the fibres. This is achieved by forcing them into closer contact by slightly twisting the roving. If, however, too much twist is used, friction between fibres becomes so high that they can no longer be drawn, and drafting becomes difficult or impossible. The control of these two simple operations forms the basis of all spinning from staple fibres.

2. THE BASIC PRINCIPLES AND PROCESSES OF SPINNING

The essential actions of drafting, i.e., drawing fibres from a sliver or roving, inserting twist to form a yarn and then winding the yarn on to a spindle or bobbin, are common to all methods of spinning. Where drawing and twisting are a separate operation from winding on, the spinning process is intermittent. Where they take place at the same time the spinning is continuous.

Intermittent spinning processes

When yarns are spun by hand, using a drop spindle or spinning wheel, the actions of drafting and twisting take place at more or less the same time.

Thus as a softly twisted roving is extended and twisted, the thinner places will take up most twist. In these thinner places the friction between fibres will become so high that fibre movement is impossible and drafting will stop. Drafting will then only continue in the thicker places until they too are thin enough to take twist and stop drafting. It seems, therefore, that as the roving is drawn and twisted, the twist is continually redistributed along the yarn as it is formed and that the actions of simultaneously drafting and twisting should result in a levelling out of uneven places in the yarn. This is apparently what happens in practice although it is only true to a certain extent. The control of drafting in this way, by means of twist, is called spindle drafting.

The simplest and oldest method of spinning is an intermittent one using the drop spindle, in India called a takli. This simple device, which has been used for thousands of years, takes the form of a short stick forming the spindle, and a weight or whorl. There are many sizes and types, depending upon the type of fibre being spun, but the method of use is the same. A short length of yarn is twisted by hand, wound round the centre of the spindle and carried to the tip where it is hooked round a notch. The spindle is then rotated by twisting between thumb and finger, and the yarn becomes twisted.

The twisted yarn runs back to where the sliver is held in the other hand and the spinner draws fibre from the sliver to form a yarn of the required thickness and at the same time twists the spindle. Once a length of yarn has been spun, it is wound on to the spindle near the whorl and the whole process is repeated.

The quality of the yarn, in terms of evenness, thickness and strength, depends upon the skill with which the spinner can control the two actions of drawing and twisting. The type of spindle, its weight in particular, is chosen to suit the fibre being spun. A spindle for short staple cotton will be small and light, one for coarse animal hairs, such as goat or yak, will be much heavier.

Indeed, when spinning fine yarns in cotton, the weight of the spindle is taken off the yarn by allowing the lower end to rest in a smooth cup or shell so that the tension in the yarn is only that which is required to keep the spindle upright.

With long wool or flax, the fibres are usually combed out straight and tied loosely to the end of a stick, called a distaff, which is carried under one armpit

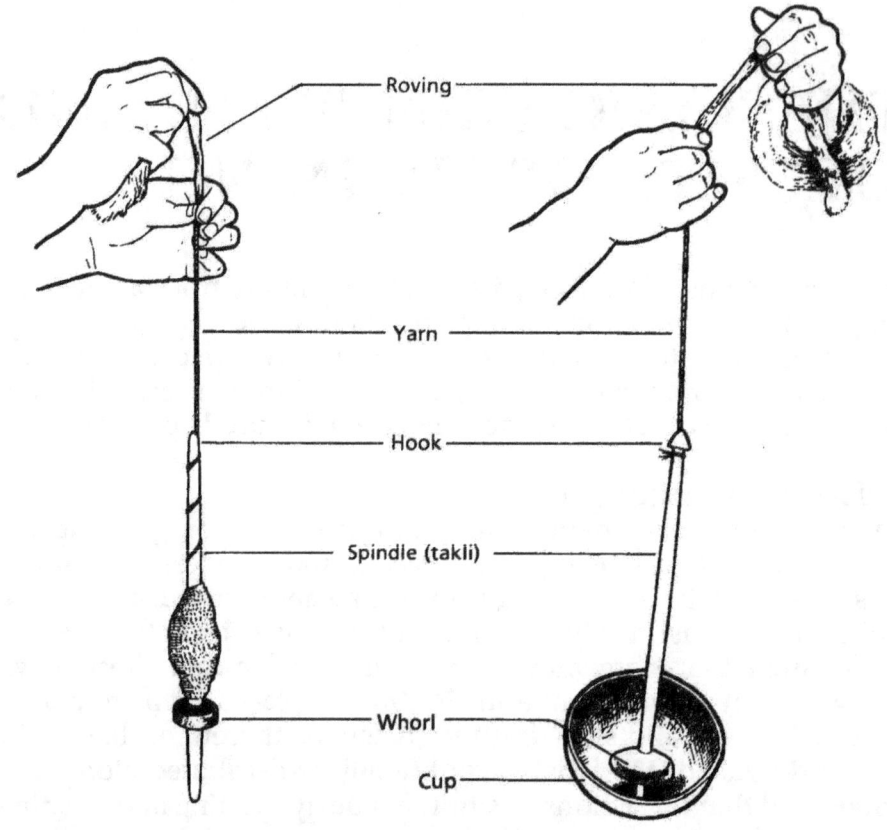

Illustration 1 Drop spindles

while spinning. In the case of cotton or short wool, the fibres in the combed sliver can easily be held in one hand while spinning.

Spinning with a simple drop spindle cannot be considered an efficient method of yarn manufacture, either in quality or quantity, especially when fine yarns are being spun. The principal advantage is that the spindle can be used anywhere, standing, walking about, tending sheep etc. An experienced spinner might expect to produce about 60-110 metres of 120 Tex woollen yarn in an hour (approximately 15-20 grams). (The usual term used to describe yarn thickness is the 'count'. In this manual the Tex system is used: see Chapter 3.) For some of the above reasons, the simple spinning wheel became a logical development of the drop spindle. This spindle is laid on its side and mounted between bearings, and the whorl is replaced by a pulley which is driven by a band or string running round a large wheel. In India this is the traditional charkha which is used while sitting on the ground. In Europe, the wheel is mounted on a stand and the spinner sits on a chair. There are many variations on the simple spinning wheel and thousands are still in use throughout the world (see illustrations 2,3 and 4).

In use the yarn is attached to the spindle as before, but held at a slight angle to it. As the wheel rotates, the yarn spirals up it until it reaches the tip, where it slips off, each time inserting one turn of twist. The sliver or roving is again held in one hand and as the wheel is turned, fibres are drafted from the roving, which is steadily drawn away from the spindle until a length of yarn has been formed which is as long as the spinner's reach. The spindle is now stopped and then briefly reversed to take the yarn off the point (backing-off).

Illustration 2 Indian charkha

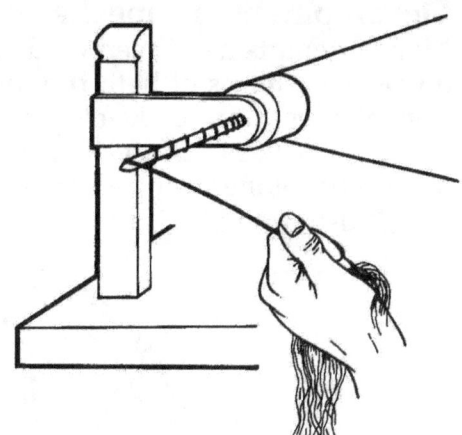
Illustration 3 The spindle (detail)

Illustration 4 English great wheel

The hand holding the roving with the attached yarn is then brought across at right angles to the spindle, which is again rotated to wind the yarn on to it. The process is then repeated so that spinning becomes an intermittent process of drafting/twisting, backing-off, winding on, drafting/twisting, etc.

The quality of the yarn in terms of fineness and evenness of twist depends entirely upon the skill of the spinner. However, the simple spinning wheel is much more productive than the drop spindle and an experienced spinner might expect to make about 10 grams of 33 Tex cotton yarn per hour.

Developments in mechanization

Many attempts have been made to make intermittent spinning processes more efficient, in terms of both the quality and the quantity of yarn produced. The first of these was a development by James Hargreaves called the spinning jenny. This was in effect a hand-operated mechanical device which imitated the actions of spinner using a simple spinning wheel, but which had many spindles (see Illustration 5).

Illustration 5 Spinning jenny

This was followed by a development in 1779 by Samuel Crompton called the mule. In this machine, fibres for spinning were drawn from a roving by means of roller drafting, but then spindle drafting and twisting were used to make a very fine and even yarn.

This machine was developed for many years to a very high level, but was gradually replaced by developments in continuous spinning, such as ring spinning, and these days the mule is only used for the production of high quality speciality yarns, using modern electronic control systems. However it was always an intermittent spinning method and in the end could not compete with developments in continuous spinning for large-scale yarn manufacture.

Continuous spinning processes

There would be an obvious advantage if the three actions of spinning, namely drafting, twisting and winding on, could take place concurrently. The basic invention which allowed this to take place was the development of the spindle and flyer mechanism as an addition to the traditional spinning wheel. This development first started in Europe in the fifteenth century and was used mostly to spin long-fibre materials such as wool, hemp and flax; it was not used for short-fibre material such as cotton. This method of spinning proved very important, as the principles involved have led to all the later methods of continuous mechanical spinning.

The spindle and pulley arrangement of the traditional spinning wheel or 'charkha' is modified so that the end of the spindle is hollow for a short distance, with another hole at right angles part way down the spindle. Yarn can pass throughout the hollow spindle and out of the side hole, so that as the spindle rotates the yarn must also rotate and thus twist is inserted; the yarn is not attached to the spindle as it would be on the traditional spinning wheel.

Once the yarn has been twisted, all that is needed is a means of collecting the yarn and winding it on to a bobbin of some kind. This is achieved by the addition of a flyer, a horseshoe-shaped piece of metal or wood attached to the spindle near the side hole.

The arms of the flyer are slotted at intervals or may carry hooks, so that the twisted yarn, after leaving the side hole in the spindle, is taken up to one arm of the flyer, hooked through a slot and then down to a bobbin which runs freely on the spindle.

As the spindle and flyer rotate, yarn is wound on to the bobbin. At intervals during spinning the yarn is moved to another slot in the flyer arm so that it builds up evenly on the bobbin. To draw the yarn through the hollow spindle, over the flyer and on to the bobbin, the bobbin must turn more slowly than the spindle.

This is usually achieved by slowing down the rotation of the bobbin by a brake band running in a groove at one end; the tension in the band, which is controllable, creates drag on the bobbin and thus also in the yarn. On some spinning wheels the yarn bobbin is positively driven by the same band which drives the spindle by doubling it round the large driving wheel. Because the bobbin pulley is smaller than the spindle pulley it is driven faster and so pulls the yarn on to the bobbin.

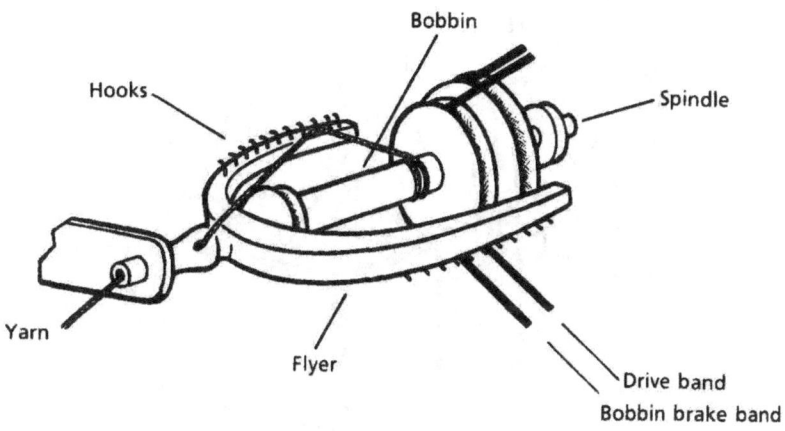

Illustration 6 Driven bobbin

In this type of spinning wheel, because the bobbin rotates at a constant speed, the speed at which yarn is drawn on to it increases as yarn builds up on the bobbin. Thus the twist in the yarn will decrease as the bobbin fills and the spinner must deliver more drafted fibre.

To compensate for this, the drive band to the bobbin is adjusted to give a controlled degree of slip.

There are many variations on this basic mechanism but the principle of operation remains the same for all spindle and flyer spinning wheels.

A final improvement is that the driving wheel is treadle operated, leaving both hands free to control the drafting of the fibres. Because of this greater control and the more uniform action of continuously twisting and winding on, it is possible to make yarns which are much more uniform in evenness and twist than with a traditional charkha. The final quality of the yarn, however, still depends to a large extent upon the skill with which the spinner controls the evenness and speed of drafting in relation to the spindle speed. Illustrations 9a and 9b are treadle - operated spinning wheels. On these, the yarn is guided on to the bobbin by a ring and traveller mechanism.

Because of the continuous operation, spinning is also more productive compared to a traditional charkha. An experienced spinner might expect to produce about 300 metres of 200 Tex woollen yarn per hour (approximately 60 grams), or 215 metres of 60 Tex yarn (approximately 14 grams).

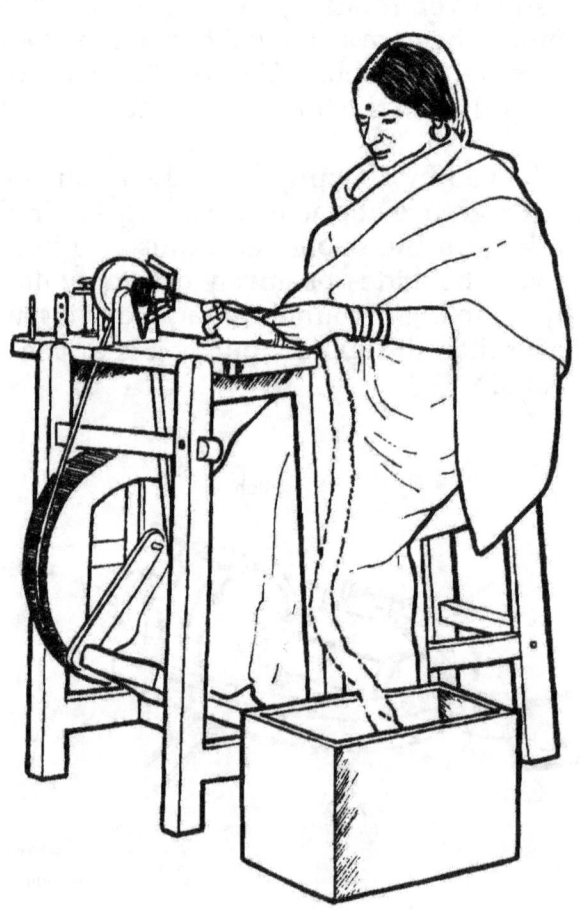

Illustration 7 Indian Bageshwar charkha

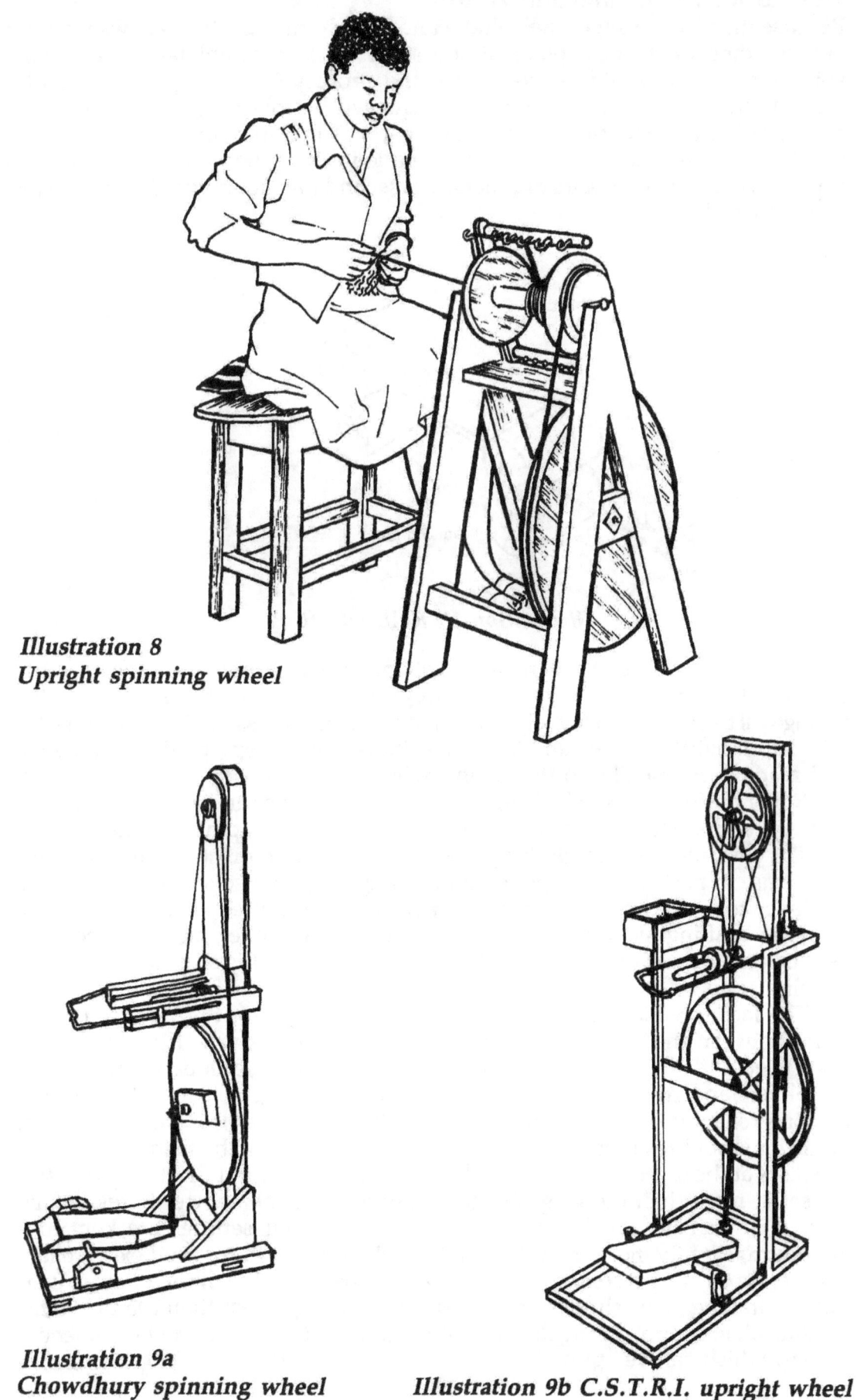

Illustration 8
Upright spinning wheel

Illustration 9a
Chowdhury spinning wheel

Illustration 9b C.S.T.R.I. upright wheel

Developments in mechanization

Because the mechanism of the spindle and flyer spinning wheel allows twisting and winding on to take place at the same time, a completely mechanized spinning system would be possible if the process of drafting could also be carried out mechanically. This can be achieved by roller drafting, and in this case drafting and twisting are separate parts of the spinning process.

The basis of roller drafting is very simple in that when the sliver or roving is passed between two pairs of rollers, the second pair are revolving at a greater speed than the first.

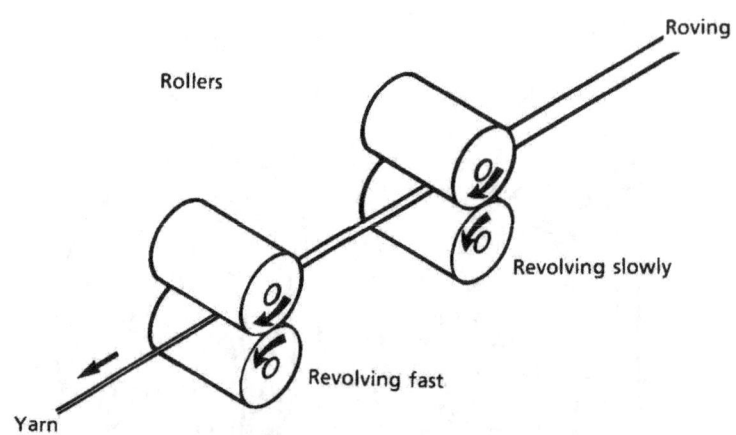

Illustration 10 Roller drafting

If the second pair of rollers are revolving at, say, eight times the speed of the first, the fibres will be drawn through at eight times the speed and the roving will be reduced to one-eighth of its original thickness, giving what is called a 'draft of eight'. At the same time the fibres will be separated, straightened and made to lie parallel to the roving axis.

Roller drafting is used both in pre-spinning, in sliver and roving formation, and as the first stage of spinning on ring, cap or flyer spinning frames.

The basic idea of roller drafting is very simple, but in practice there are some problems. In particular, simple systems using only two sets of rollers, have a tendency to create irregularities in the roving being drafted. Therefore, almost all roller drafting systems use additional rollers, or other means of control, between the driven ones to control fibre movement in this area, known as the drafting zone.

The factors which affect the evenness of drafting are: the setting, i.e. the space between the two sets of driven rollers (sometimes called the ratch), the draft used and the fibre length. All three factors are interdependent.

Slivers and rovings contain fibres of different lengths. The setting of the drafting rollers is therefore critical. If the rollers are set at less than the length of the longest fibres present, both ends of the fibres would be held by both sets of rollers at the same time and the fibres would break or not draft. If the rollers are set at more than the length of the longest fibres the shorter fibres will be drafted in far from ideal conditions. In practice roller settings are kept to a minimum, slightly more than the length of the longest fibres, and extra rollers or other types of fibre control systems are used between the draw rollers to control the drafting of the shorter fibres. Very short fibres, of less than 20mm length, are difficult to control during drafting and determine to a large extent the fineness of yarn which can be spun.

If long fibres are present there is a greater overlap between fibres to give friction and strength, which means that less twist is needed to make yarns of comparable strength with longer fibres than is needed with short fibres. Table 1 shows the effect of fibre length on the thickness of yarn which can be spun.

STAPLE LENGTH	YARN COUNTS
Up to 22mm	Up to 30 Tex
22 to 28mm	Up to 20 Tex
28 to 32mm	20 to 12 Tex
32 to 36mm	Up to 10 Tex

Table 1 Cotton yarn counts spun from specific staple lengths

The effect of draft is also important: too high a draft in relation to fibre length makes the drafting very uneven. In simple roller drafting systems, drafts of up to six or seven may be used for spinning, as this would allow fewer drawing processes to be used in preparing the roving or even enable them to be omitted them altogether.

To use higher drafts it is necessary to control the movement of fibres between the drafting rollers very carefully, and a number of high draft systems have been developed to do this. All of them increase the degree of fibre packing between the drafting rollers by a variety of methods. By using systems of this type, drafts as high as twenty to forty can be used with some fibres.

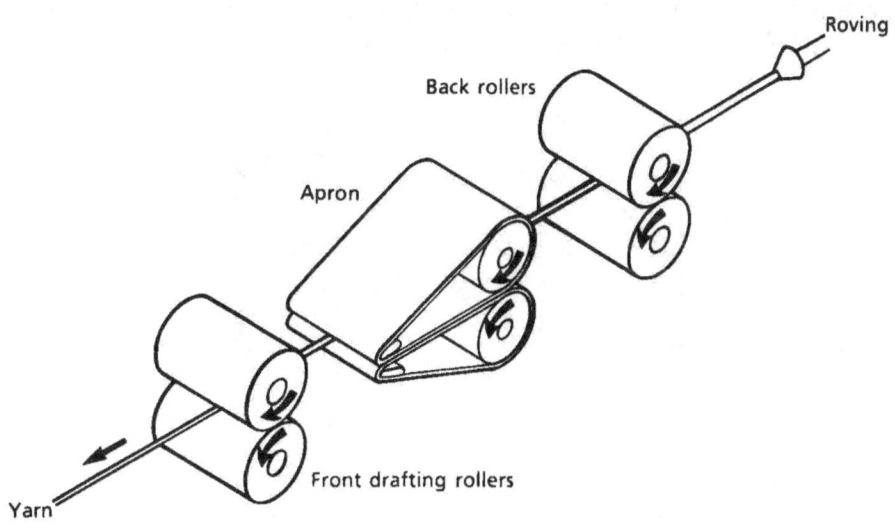

Illustration 11 High draft system for ring spinning

When the roving of fibres has been drafted to the weight per unit length needed to make a yarn of the required thickness and it leaves the front drafting rollers, it is twisted. Twisting the fibres together increases the friction between fibres and thus the yarn strength. The amount of twist is determined by the fibre properties (mostly fibre length), the thickness (count) and the intended use of the yarn.

If the amount of twist in a yarn is gradually increased, friction between fibres increases and the yarn becomes stronger. Eventually a point is reached when no amount of additional twist will make the yarn any stronger, indeed it will start to get weaker.

In practice, the amount of twist is decided by the end use of the yarn. Warp yarns, for example, which need to be strong and elastic to withstand the strains of weaving, are given more twist than weft yarns, which need to be softly twisted and bulky to give good "cover" and which are not normally subjected to much tension. For special qualities in the yarn the twist used may be more than that needed to provide maximum strength, for example in yarns for crepe fabrics.

A useful measure of the twist hardness of a yarn, is a number called the 'twist factor' (twist multiplier).

This is obtained in the following manner:

Twist Factor (measured in any indirect yarn count system such as cotton)

= Twist (T.P.I) divided by the square root of the yarn count.

OR, Twist Factor (measured in any direct yarn count system, e.g. Tex).

= Twist (T.P.I) multiplied by the square root of the yarn count.

(In this manual, twist is measured in turns per inch (T.P.I), which is used in all twist calculations. Sometimes, twist factors are given which have been calculated on the basis of turns per metre (T.P.M) or turns per centimetre (T.P.Cm).)

The twist factor is a useful measure of the character of a yarn, since it is approximately proportional to the angle of twist of the fibres in the yarn. Thus a high twist factor will indicate a yarn with a high angle of twist which will be hard and probably strong. A low twist factor will indicate a softer and probably weaker yarn.

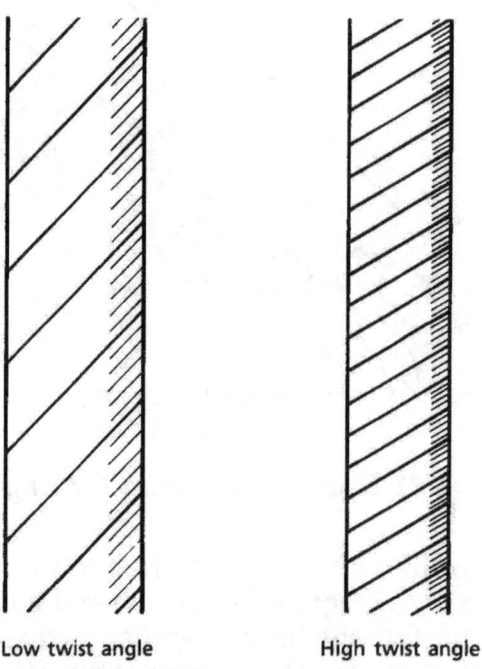

Low twist angle   High twist angle

Illustration 12 Angle of twist

Since all fibres differ in their frictional properties, the twist factor can only give an approximate idea of yarn character; in practice, twist factors are chosen for particular yarns which experience has shown to be good for the material being spun and the end use of the yarn.

Twist factors are, however, very useful as a measure of quality control. Any variation in twist factor between different lots of the same yarn may show in the finished fabric and affect the evenness of appearance. This is particularly true during dyeing and finishing especially if the fabric is to be brushed or raised. Appendices 1 and 2 show the relationship between yarn count, twist and twist factor for woollen and cotton yarns.

At this point it is important to note one basic difference between spinning methods which use spindle drafting and those which use roller drafting. As has already been pointed out, when drafting and twisting take place at the same time, there is a tendency to even out any thick or thin places in the yarn as it is spun. Since spindle drafting these days is almost entirely limited to hand spinning methods, a further factor enters - the skill of the spinner; a very skilful spinner can make a surprisingly even yarn.

However, when roller drafting is used, for example during ring spinning, once the roving has been drafted, twisting is a separate operation and there is almost no tendency to even out thick or thin places. Evenness in this case depends entirely upon the evenness of the drafted roving, and the skill of the spinner can play no part in making the yarn more even. Indeed when spinning highly twisted yarns on ring spinning frames, any unevenness in the roving will be emphasized by the twist running to the thin places. To obtain a very even yarn appearance with ring-spun yarns, it is often advantageous to use the lowest possible twist factor consistent with obtaining all the other values, e.g. strength.

When spinning yarns on ring, cap or flyer spinning frames, the evenness of the roving from which the yarn is spun is thus very important and in this case skill is needed to adjust the draw frames and spinning frames to give the best possible values for the fibres being spun.

Methods of twisting

In the case of yarns which are spun by intermittent methods, for example by hand using a drop spindle or spinning wheel with a simple spindle, the drafted rovings are twisted by the rotation of the spindle, one turn of the spindle inserting one turn of twist in the yarn.

In effect, one end of the yarn is held and the other end rotated until the desired degree of twist is obtained, then the length of twisted yarn is wound on to the spindle. The number of turns per inch (T.P.I) in the yarn is the number of turns made by the spindle divided by the length of yarn which is twisted. Since, in practice, both these values are difficult to measure, the twist in the yarn remains a matter of judgement by the spinner. Again a skilful spinner can make a yarn in which the twist is reasonably consistent.

In the case of yarns spun by continuous spinning methods, the principle used to twist the yarn is that if one end is held and the other end swung round in a circular path, the yarn will be twisted, one turn of twist being inserted for each rotation. The methods used to control the movement of yarn in a circular path vary, but the principle is the same for all continuous spinning systems.

After the yarn has been moved in a circular path to insert twist, it is wound on to a bobbin or some other type of collector, and in this case, twisting and winding on take place simultaneously. The number of turns per inch in the yarn in this case can be calculated approximately, by dividing the number of turns per minute made by the twist insertion mechanism, by the speed in inches per minute of yarn delivery from the front drafting rollers. Both these values can be measured fairly easily.

The first completely mechanized continuous spinning system was the water-driven frame developed by Richard Arkwright in 1760, which was essentially a series of spindle and flyer spinning heads with roller drafting for the fibre roving.

All later developments in continuous spinning have come from these basic mechanisms. Many improvements have taken place in the methods of drafting the fibres to be spun, in speed of yarn production and in the size of package on which the spun yarn is collected, but the basic principles of yarn production are all essentially similar.

In practice, there are four methods by which twist is inserted in the yarn before it is wound on to a bobbin:

(1) Flyer spinning

This is the most obvious and direct development of the spindle and flyer spinning wheel. The fibre roving is drafted between pairs of rollers running at different speeds, usually with some type of additional fibre control method between the front and back rollers. The drafted fibres are led through a guide immediately above the spindle carrying the bobbin and twist is inserted by passing the yarn through the hollow top of the flyer, round one leg and then on to the bobbin on which it is wound. The bobbin is carried on a rail which rises and falls to distribute the spun yarn evenly. To control the amount of twist inserted accurately, the spindle and flyer are driven at a constant speed so that, as with the spindle and flyer spinning wheel, the bobbin must rotate at a slower speed so that yarn is wound on. This is achieved either by slowing down the bobbin rotation by means of a friction pad underneath it, or by driving it separately at a variable speed to allow for the increase in diameter of the bobbin as the yarn builds up.

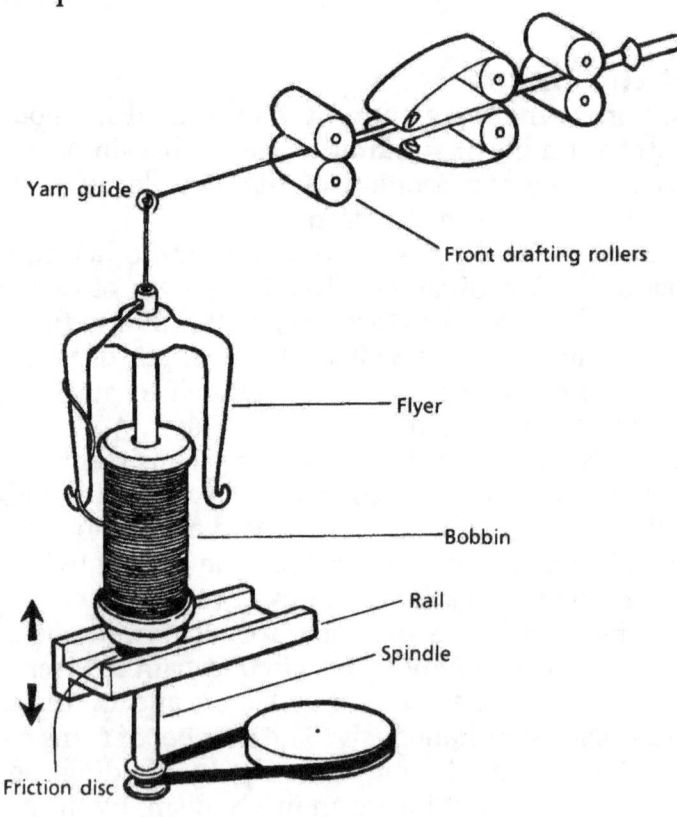

Illustration 13 Flyer spinning

Flyer spinning is not used much these days for producing yarns, but flyer type frames are used as a means of reducing the thickness of slivers to produce rovings for spinning by another method. Flyer spinning has the advantage that because the roving passes round the leg of the flyer and is thus supported by it, it is not subjected to as much stress as it would be if a different method was used, e.g. ring spinning.

(2) Cap spinning

When cap spinning was developed it represented the first really significant change in methods of twisting and winding on. The fibre roving is again drafted between pairs of rollers and the drafted fibres are led through a guide immediately above the spindle carrying the bobbin. The yarn is guided on to the bobbin by passing round the base of a stationary cap, twist is inserted by the rotation of the bobbin, causing the yarn to rotate around the spindle, and the friction or drag of the yarn on the cap causes it to wind on to the bobbin. The bobbin is again carried on a rail which rises and falls to distribute the yarn evenly. The spindle runs at a constant speed and the amount of twist inserted can be controlled by varying the speed at which the roving leaves the front draw rollers.

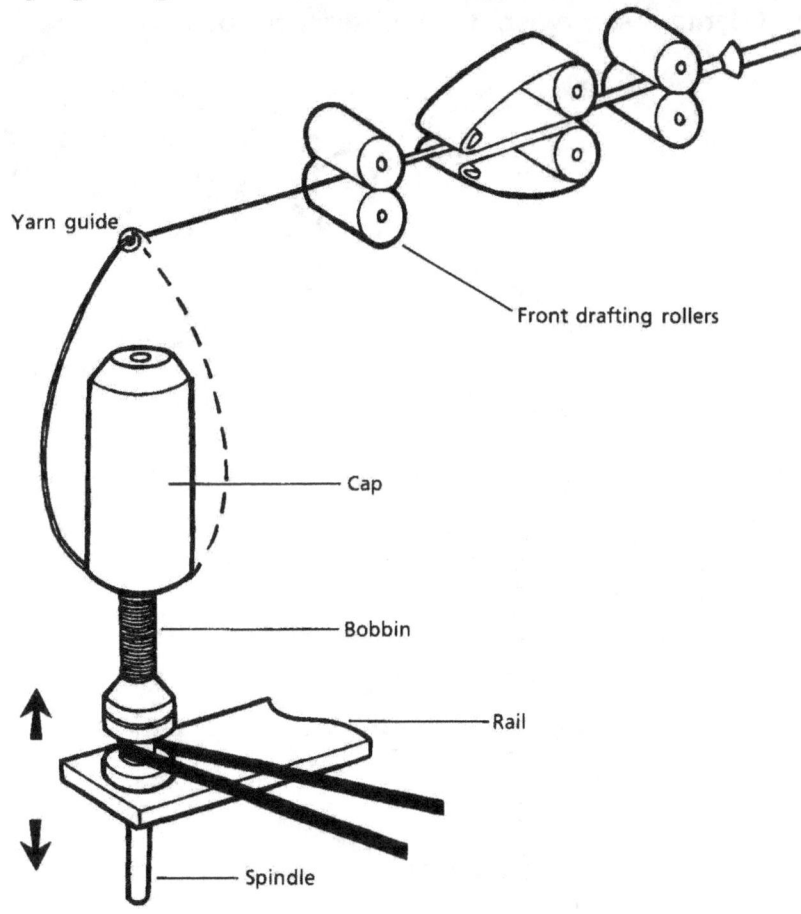

Illustration 14 Cap spinning

Cap spinning has now been almost entirely superseded by ring spinning, one of its main disadvantages being that to remove the full bobbin of yarn (doffing), it was necessary to remove the cap from the spindle, and the cap limited the size of spinning bobbin.

(3) Ring spinning

After its introduction in 1830, ring spinning became the dominant method of spinning staple fibres. The principle, which is very simple, is similar to cap spinning except that the yarn is guided on to the spinning bobbin by a ring and traveller arrangement rather than the edge of a cap.

After leaving the front draw rollers the drafted fibres are again led through a guide immediately above the spindle carrying the bobbin. Twist is again inserted by the bobbin rotation and the yarn is guided on to the bobbin by a C-shaped piece of wire, called the traveller, which is loosely clipped on to the flange of a ring mounted round the bobbin. The traveller is pulled round the ring by the yarn, inserting one turn of twist for each revolution. At the same time the friction of the traveller on the ring causes it to lag behind the revolving bobbin by an amount sufficient to wind the yarn on to the bobbin. The amount of twist inserted is again controlled by varying the speed at which the roving leaves the front draw rollers.

Although the ring spinning machine is very simple and is capable of spinning high quality yarns to a wide range of counts, in industrial terms it has probably reached its peak of development. This is for the fundamental reason that, in order to insert twist, it is necessary to rotate the fairly heavy bobbin of

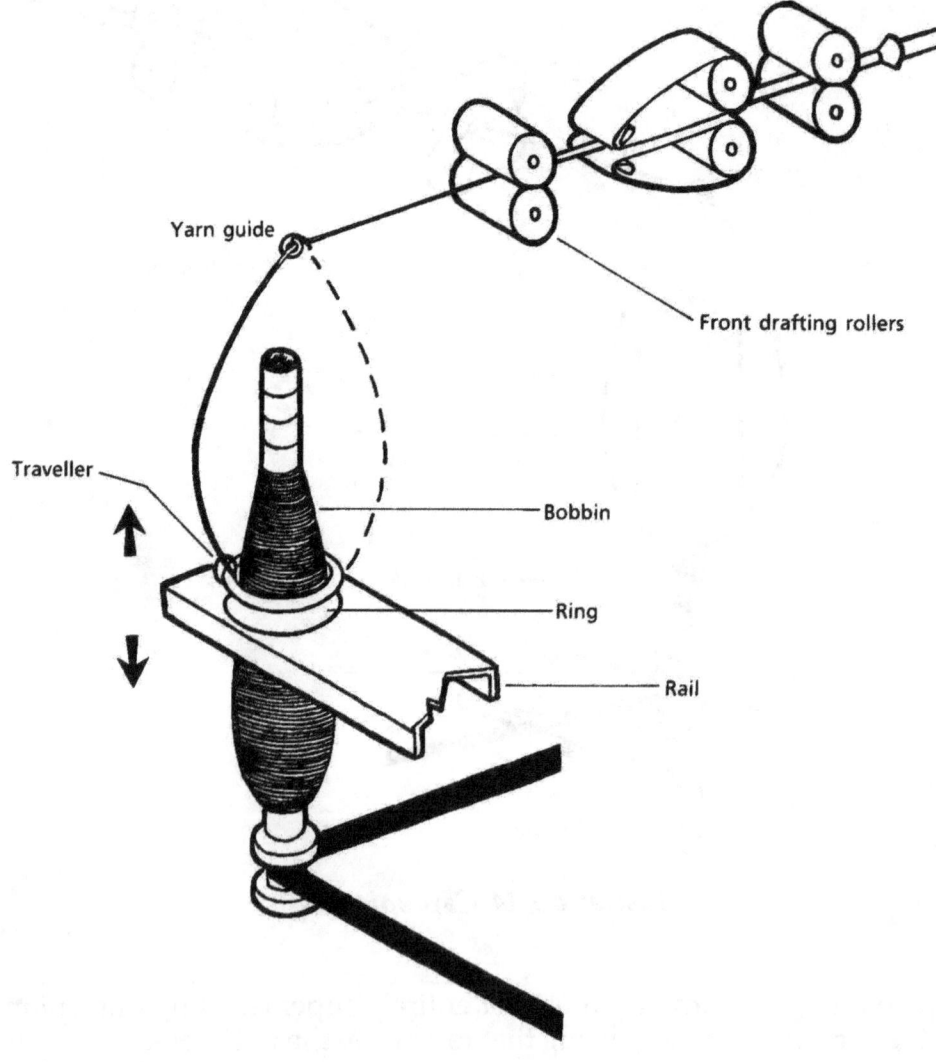

Illustration 15 Ring spinning

yarn and this consumes a lot of power. Any attempt to increase productivity by increasing spindle speed or bobbin size requires so much extra power that the process becomes uneconomic. These reasons are not as valid, of course, for small scale manually-operated ring spinning machines, but even here eight spindles are about the maximum number which can be hand operated, up to twelve require foot-pedal operation and more than twelve need to be power-driven.

These problems have led to the development of spinning methods which do not rely upon the rotation of a heavy bobbin to insert twist. Some of these are of interest for small scale spinning and one or two have been modified and developed for hand operation.

(4) Centrifugal or pot spinning

In this spinning process the drafted fibres, after leaving the front draw rollers, pass down a vertical guide tube which leads into an open-topped pot. The pot rotates at high speed, the rotation inserts twist and the yarn is collected on the inside of the pot. The guide tube moves up and down to distribute the yarn evenly in the pot.

The tensions on the yarn as it is being formed are much less than in ring spinning and so spinning speeds can be higher by a factor of two or three. The output of yarn is about three times that of a hand-operated ring spindle and with a good drafting system the yarn can be spun directly from carefully prepared slivers, eliminating the need to make rovings.

There are some disadvantages, mostly that is is only possible to spin fairly coarse yarns, up to 40 Tex, and the yarn must be removed from the pot by a separate process. The pot must also always rotate or the contents will collapse.

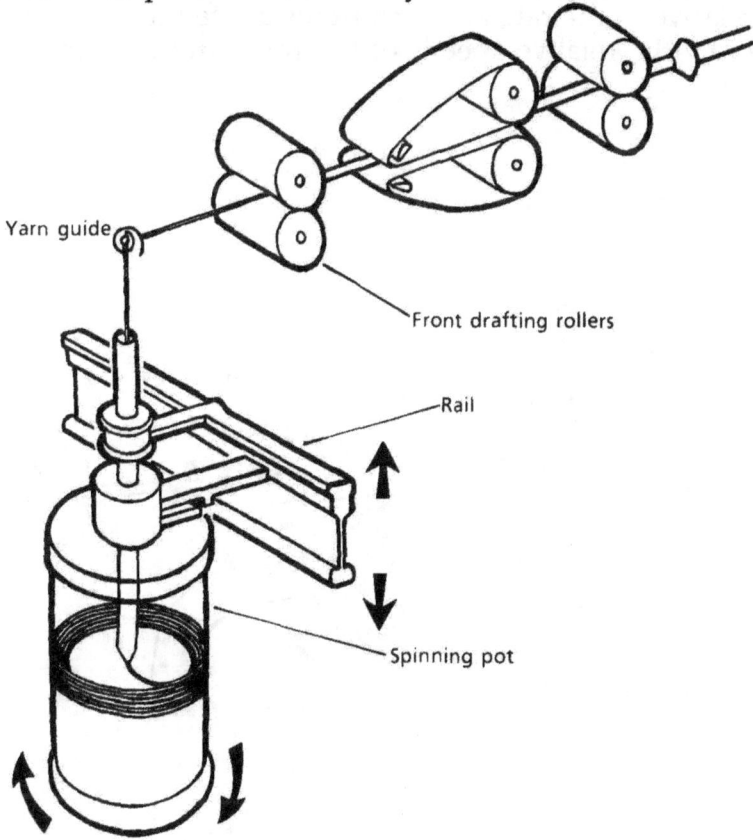

Illustration 16 Pot spinning

(5) Rotor spinning

This relatively new method of spinning is one method of open-end or break spinning. It relies upon a completely different principle of yarn formation and twist insertion to that used in ring or pot spinning. The disadvantages of these processes, rotating a heavy bobbin or removing the yarn from the pot as a separate operation, could be overcome if a method could be developed to twist the strand of fibres as it is formed without the need to rotate a bobbin or pot. This is achieved in rotor spinning by introducing a gap or break in the flow of fibres between the drafting rollers (or other delivery method) and the final yarn package and by introducing twist merely by rotating the strand at the break or open-end. Thus twisting and winding on become separate operations. The twisting element (rotor) can be very small and compact and because only a small amount of fibre is being twisted at any one moment, very high twisting speeds can be used and the yarn can be wound separately on to a package of any size or type.

The basic principles of rotor spinning are shown in Illustration 17. A continuous supply of fibres from either drafting rollers or an opening unit is sucked down a fibre delivery tube and deposited in the groove of the rotor where it is held in place by its rapid rotation.

The fibre layer in the rotor groove is continuously peeled off and twisted to form a yarn which passes through the trumpet of the delivery tube and is wound on to any type of package.

At the point at which the fibre layer is peeled from the rotor groove and twisted, it is moving steadily anti-clockwise and the rotor is moving at very high speed past the fibre delivery tube.

The count of the yarn is determined by the rate at which yarn is drawn out of the rotor relative to the rate at which fibres are fed in. The amount of twist is determined by the relative speeds of the rotor and of yarn delivery.

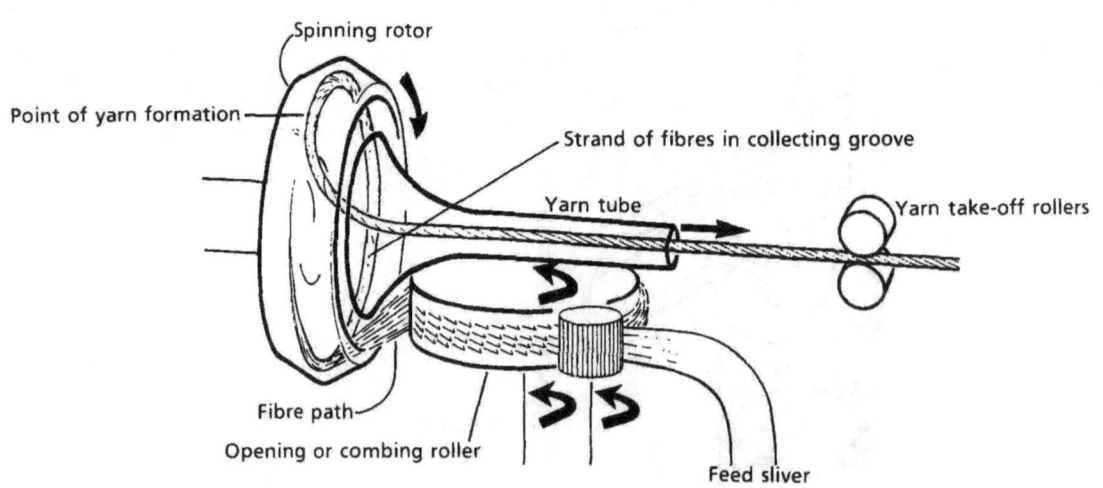

Illustration 17 Basic principles of rotor spinning

There are many types of rotor spinning machines, but the supply of fibres to the rotor is achieved in one of two ways:

(a) By the use of normal drafting rollers, as on the ring frame.

(b) By the use of an opening unit using a combing roller.

Fibres in the form of a sliver are fed by means of a small feed roller to the rapidly rotating combing roller which is covered with wire points. This detaches fibres from the sliver and projects them into the airstream, down the delivery tube and so to the spinning rotor.

The opening unit has the advantage that it is fed by a fibre sliver, which means that some of the preparatory processes can be omitted. The unit can also be modified to remove any particles of trash left in the sliver after the pre-spinning processes. This also helps to keep the rotor clean when spinning low grade cotton.

Yarns produced by rotor spinning have a very different character from those produced by ring or pot spinning. In general, the fibres in ring-spun yarns have been through several drawing processes and on leaving the front draw rollers are in a parallel state which is maintained as the yarn is twisted and wound on to the spinning bobbin.

During rotor spinning, the 'break' in the sliver allows the fibres to relax even as they are laid in the rotor groove and they are then twisted in this relaxed state. This makes rotor-spun yarn bulkier and more extensible than ring-spun yarn of equivalent counts. The effect of laying the fibres in layers in the rotor groove also reduces the variation in the number of fibres in the yarn cross-section and the result is a much more regular yarn.

It is also only possible to spin fairly coarse yarns, in the range 20-300 Tex on large power-driven machines with high rotor speeds and 100-300 Tex on small hand-operated machines with lower rotor speeds.

Although there are many other differences between rotor-spun and ring-spun yarns, particularly in the economics of large scale production, in general rotor-spun yarns in comparison with ring spun yarns are:

- (a) more uniform in appearance
- (b) less variable in strength
- (c) not as strong
- (d) more extensible
- (e) bulkier
- (f) more absorbent
- (g) more abrasion resistant

Newer methods of making yarns

1. Wrap spinning

This is a yarn production in which a conventionally spun yarn is bound or wrapped with another yarn or continuous filament.

When spinning yarns from staple fibres using conventional machinery, it is necessary to twist the fibres together to increase friction between them and so increase strength. If another yarn or filament is wrapped around the core of staple fibres, the friction between fibres is increased by the wrapping yarn and it is then possible to make strong yarns with low twist.

The strength of the yarn is also increased by the addition of the filament. It is thus possible by this simple process to produce yarns with good properties for a wide range of applications.

Wrap yarns are now made on a wide range of spinning machines, but are probably most successful when made on machinery which is specially suited or adapted to the purpose, such as hollow spindle or twistless spinning systems. However, they can be made successfully on more conventional machinery and are of considerable interest for small scale manufacturers using simple equipment.

The advantages of wrap-spun yarns are:

(a) All types of spun yarns can be wrapped.

(b) Because of the fibre friction produced by wrapping, it is possible to make strong yarns with less twist than would normally be neccessary and the yarns have a softer handle and more bulk.

(c) Because of the wrapping yarn, it is possible to spin fine yarns from relatively coarse fibres and waste material can be made into useful yarn.

(d) Wrap-spun yarns are generally stronger and more elastic than conventionally spun yarns; for example, cotton warp yarns can be made which do not need sizing.

One disadvantage of wrap spun yarn is that, because the final yarn contains two components, one of which may be a filament yarn, problems could occur in dyeing and finishing, and sometimes the filament may show in an undesirable manner in the finished fabric.

Methods of wrap spinning

Wrap spun yarns can be made on most types of ring spinning machines. The wrapping yarn or filament is drawn from a bobbin situated behind the drafting mechanism on the spinning frame and threaded through the front delivery rollers so that it emerges alongside the drafted roving. Correct positioning of the filament is important and is achieved by means of a guide close to the front delivery rollers. This method can be used for the production of all types of wrap-spun cotton, wool and flax yarns.

The choice of wrapping yarn or filament depends upon the fibre content of the spun yarn and the properties required. For good strength and stretch properties a continuous filament of nylon or polyester wrapping yarn is best: these can be of fine count and so become hidden in the spun yarn. Where dying or finishing is likely to be a problem, a wrapping yarn can be used which is more compatible with the spun core, e.g. nylon or silk for wool or hair fibre spun yarns, fine cotton or rayon for cotton spun yarns etc. The most important wrapping yarns are listed below:

Filament Type	Count Range (Tex)
Nylon	17 to 228
Polyester	17 to 167
Polypropylene	78 to 330
Acrylic	78
Acetate/Viscose	220 to 330
Silk	33 to 88
Staple Yarns	50 to 2000
Water Soluble	62

Where a water soluble wrapping yarn is used, the spun yarn can have very low twist. After weaving or knitting the wrapping yarn is removed by washing to give a very soft fabric.

The relationship between the tension of the wrapping yarn and the spun core during spinning is important. If the wrapping yarn is not evenly tensioned during spinning, the uniformity and final appearance of the yarn will be badly affected. Yarns spun with too low a filament tension show hardly any constriction of the spun core, but with too high tension the core yarn becomes distorted. Best results are obtained when the core yarn is sufficiently constricted to give the required fibre friction.

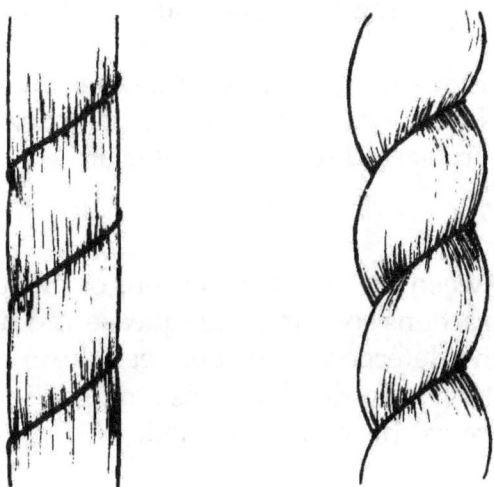

Illustration 18 Effect of wrapping filament tension

Many different effects can be obtained by exploiting the properties of more specialized wrapping yarns and different spinning systems, but these are outside the scope of this manual.

2. Yarn felting

This method of making yarn is of considerable interest for small scale manufacture since it is a simple process which eliminates the need for spinning and twisting. It does, however, require the supply of roving or slivers which can be prepared to given specifications.

The process is very simple in principle in that any yarn is made by causing the fibres in a roving to felt, that is, to become entangled and thus gain sufficient strength to form a yarn. The entanglement of the fibres increases friction between them and, in a sense, felting performs the same function as twisting in a conventionally spun yarn.

Since felting can only take place because of the unique frictional properties of wool or hair fibres, felted yarns can only be made from these fibres or from a blend of fibres containing a high proportion of wool. The final thickness and count of the yarn depends upon the roving or sliver from which it is made and since it is difficult to make very fine and regular rovings, felted yarns are usually fairly coarse (250-8000 Tex). They are therefore most suitable for carpets and rugs, although some weaving and knitting yarns are possible.

Low twist yarns made by conventional spinning methods can also be felted to give the appearance and strength characteristics of felted yarns, but in this case the process is not so useful since one of the principal advantages is the elimination of the conventional spinning operations.

Felted yarns have unique properties; in particular, the fibres in the yarn are bound together very firmly by the felting process, so that carpets, rugs or fabrics made from them retain their surface appearance for long periods. Felted yarns are strong and elastic and can be used in combination with conventionally spun yarns to make interesting effects in fabrics. They are also economical to produce since the relatively expensive processes of spinning and twisting are eliminated and in some cases yarn scouring (washing) can take place at the same time as felting.

In practice two methods of continuously felting a wollen roving or sliver have been developed. In each case the fibres in the roving are squeezed and rubbed together while immersed in warm water and/or detergent.

(a) Apron felting

The roving is passed between two revolving aprons of rubber or neoprene which also reciprocate, the two actions combining to squeeze and rub the roving causing it to felt. Warm water and detergent is fed between the aprons with the roving. The roving may pass between a series of aprons arranged so that scouring, felting and washing takes place as the yarn is formed.

(b) Tube felting

The roving is passed through a flexible plastic tube which is squeezed by rotating rollers, the squeezing and relaxing of the tube causing the fibres to felt. Warm water and detergent is passed through the tube with the roving.

3. SIMPLE METHODS OF TESTING THE QUALITY OF SPUN YARN

Testing and quality control

Yarn is almost always made to some specification. Even when made on the simplest of equipment such as a drop spindle, an attempt will be made to achieve a particular fineness and twist hardness and to obtain a degree of consistency in these qualities.

Quality control means the procedures, actions and supervision needed to make a yarn which meets a desired specification.

Testing yarn properties is carried out to discover whether a particular quality has been achieved and to provide information which can be used to make changes in production to improve yarn quality and prevent variations from a desired specification.

It might be thought that testing and quality control is really only of use in large-scale spinning operations using modern machinery and that it has little relevance to small-scale operations using hand methods or simple machinery. To some extent this is true, and certainly some of the more complex methods of testing would not be necessary. Some simple test procedures can however be useful to achieve a degree of consistency and accuracy of manufacture.

It is important to emphasize that final measure of the quality of any yarn is its performance in use. If a yarn performs satisfactorily in a particular product and meets a customer's requirements at an economic cost, then it is of good quality. There is also no point in undertaking extensive and very accurate measurement and testing for a particular yarn property if the method used to control that property during manufacture is very unreliable. Testing methods should therefore always be related to the ability to control yarn properties during manufacture, and successful quality control depends upon the co-operation of everyone concerned in yarn manufacture. All testing can be ineffective simply because the control of quality has not been encouraged in the person who is spinning, who should be given more responsibility for quality and be properly trained.

Good communication between testing personnel and the people manufacturing the yarn is important. The person responsible for testing should be capable of giving a clear and practical interpretation of test results and the action, if any, which needs to be taken. In an ideal situation the person undertaking the testing should have a complete understanding of the operating principles of any machinery used for spinning. Interpretation of test results always involves discussions with production personnel and these should be thorough, particularly where changes in machine settings are involved. Completely arbitrary changes should never be made and production personnel should have sufficient information and confidence with regard to the effect of making changes in machine settings.

Finally, quality control should always be directed to a practical end and be a natural part of the processes of yarn manufacture, not merely the collection of statistical information. Good quality control is essentially an attitude of mind in everyone concerned with yarn manufacture and takes time to develop.

Simple methods of testing

Where yarn is made by hand methods or on very simple spinning machines, there is usually so little actual control over the final qualities of the yarn that testing or measuring any of these qualities might be thought a waste of time. Most of the yarn qualities which might be tested, thickness, twist, evenness and strength, are introduced by the skill and judgement of the spinner and not as the result of machine control settings. Yet it is often desirable, even with hand-spun yarns, to have some measure of the actual qualities being introduced during spinning, even if the measure used is again a matter of judgement rather than a number or point on a graph.

It is therefore possible to use some very simple methods of testing or measuring some yarn properties, which will at least indicate where large variations are taking place and so give the spinner an opportunity to correct or change whatever is causing the variations.

However, because of the lack of basic control over most of the factors which cause variations in yarn properties, there is no point in undertaking complex or extensive testing as the results will be meaningless in terms of being able to correct or control any variability which is discovered. Such testing will of course accurately measure whatever property is being tested and the resulting figures may be of some interest, if this is all that is required.

The yarn properties which the spinner is most likely to wish to measure and control are:

(1) Thickness (count or weight per unit length)
(2) Twist
(3) Evenness
(4) Strength

(1) Thickness of the yarn

The traditional method of describing the thickness of a yarn is to weigh a stated length, which gives the count of the yarn. This must still be done if accurate comparisons or descriptions are to be made. But this implies that a reasonable length of representative yarn is available and an accurate means of weighing it. Where yarn is being spun by hand this is not always the case and for control or comparison purposes a different measure of thickness is sometimes useful.

One practical method is to judge the actual thickness of the spun yarn by winding a short length on a rod and counting the number of threads which, when wound closely on the rod will cover one inch, or any other suitable measure. With practice this method can give consistent results and can be used as a quick check during spinning.

The yarn should be wound on the rod as shown indicating the twist direction. Avoid untwisting the yarn when winding yarn round the rod.

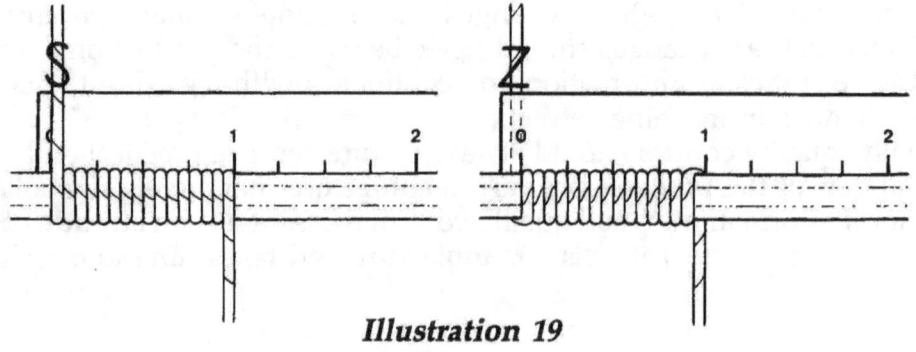

Illustration 19

An alternative method of measuring yarn thickness, but which is less accurate is to make a measuring card as shown in Illustration 20. Yarn is laid over the scales and a judgement made as to which scale it is closest. Measurements should be made at several places along the yarn to make some allowance for variations in thickness.

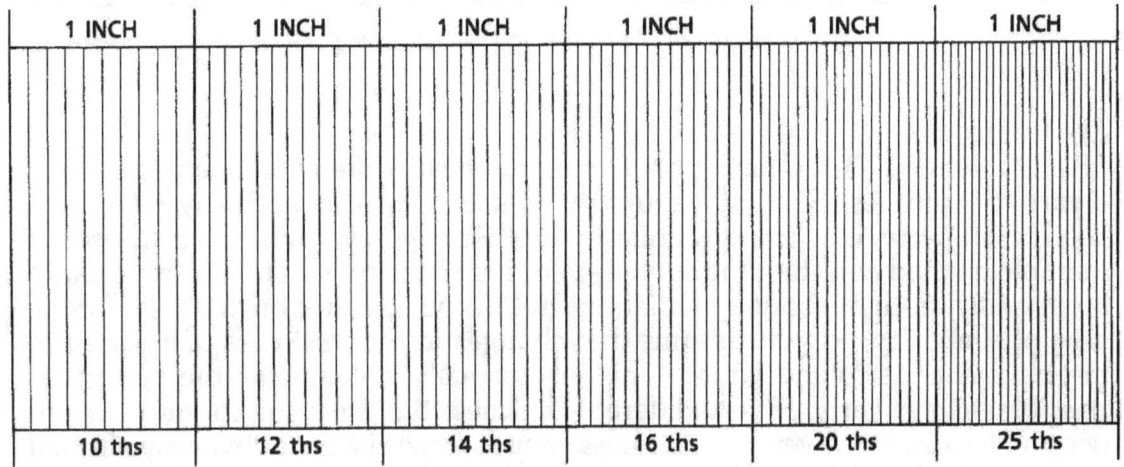

Illustration 20 Thickness-measuring card

(2) Twist

The amount of twist in a yarn plays a very important part in determining its character: in particular its hardness or softness and strength are all determined to a large extent by the amount of twist.

Variations in twist between different lots of the same yarn can have considerable effects on the final appearance of any fabric made from them and shows particularly in dying and finishing. In practice, even with well adjusted modern spinning machinery, yarns can have quite large twist variations and the same is true of hand spun yarns.

Normal methods of testing a yarn for the amount of twist involve the use of a twist testing machine, described later. If a twist testing machine is not available, simpler methods must be used and the most useful measure of the amount of twist in a yarn in this case is to estimate the angle to which the fibres in the yarn have been twisted.

This technique can be used with reasonable consistency and is a useful control method during spinning. Again, a twist angle measuring card can be made as shown in Illustration 21. The card is used by holding the yarn over the scale at exactly 0 degrees and then moving the yarn to the left or right, depending on the direction of twist, keeping the yarn parallel to the 0 degree line until the angle of twist of the fibres is the same as that of one of the degree lines. Measurements should be made at several places along the yarn to allow for variations in twist and give an average angle.

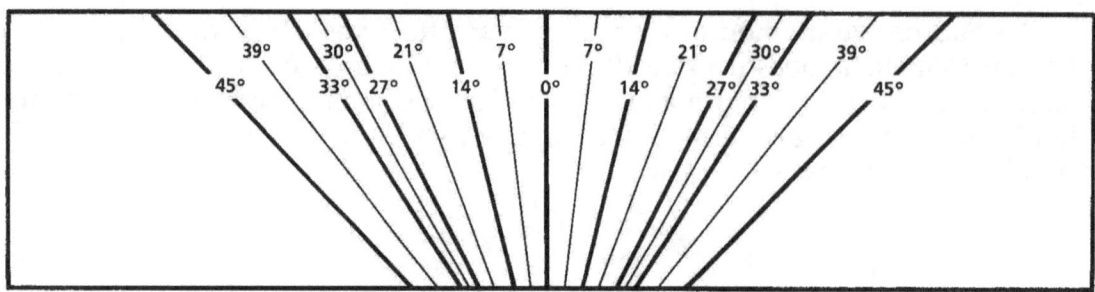

Illustration 21 Twist-angle measuring card

(3) Evenness

This is a general term which most commonly means the overall appearance of a yarn. Sometimes the term 'regularity' is used, but this normally refers to a specific property, e.g. count regularity or twist regularity. For the purposes of a simple method of testing the overall evenness of a yarn variation in appearance is generally brought about by variations in thickness, count or twist, so, for the sake of simplicity, we will assume that changes in the thickness of a yarn also means a change in the count. This is obviously not always the case: it is possible to have yarns of very different thickness but the same count or weight per unit length. However, the evenness of appearance is more obviously affected by variations in thickness than in count and this is the property which can be tested most easily in a simple way.

The evenness of appearance of a yarn can be judged most easily by winding a length on an inspection board. This is simply a board of thin plywood or rigid cardboard, about 25 by 15 centimetres, which has a smooth surface painted matt black. The yarn is wound on the board with even tension, and the spacing of the yarns is adjusted so that the space between each strand is about the same as the yarn thickness. It is important that the strands are as evenly spaced as possible and to achieve this it is best to prepare the board with a series of small notches along two edges to locate the yarn accurately. A series of boards will be needed for yarns of different thickness. Boards of standard yarns of known commercial quality may be wound and kept, or photographed, for use as standards or for comparison.

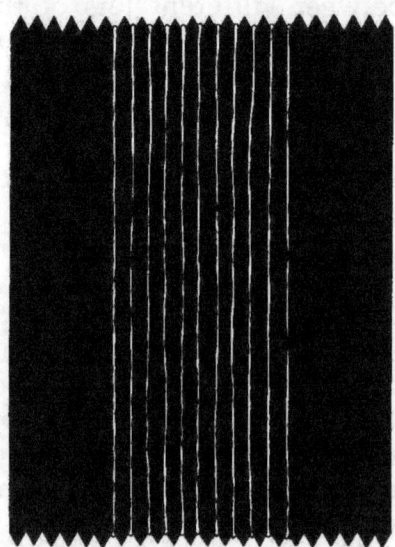

Illustration 22 Yarn inspection board

The board is examined from a short distance and a judgement made about the overall appearance, the number of thick and thin places and the number of slubs or neps (small entangled bundles of fibres trapped in the yarn).

If the number of each type of variation in the yarn on the board is counted, the numbers obtained can be used as a method of comparing yarns, although since the numbers were obtained by making judgements, they can only be of some value if the same person makes the comparison. With experience and practice yarn examination on a board can provide useful quality control information.

(4) Strength

The strength of a spun yarn is determined by many factors, from the type of fibre to the method and evenness of the spinning process. The measurement of yarn strength, with any degree of accuracy, is not possible without the use of relatively complicated testing equipment.

Summary

The simple testing methods described so far will, if used consistently and sensibly, give some degree of control over the quality of yarns produced by hand spinning or by the use of simple spinning machines. Since all the methods described rely upon a degree of judgement by the person carrying out the test, care is necessary in interpreting any results. If a series of tests is to be carried out it is best if only one person is responsible for the interpretation of results in order to give some consistency. Above all it must be possible to communicate the results of any tests to the person responsible for spinning, who must be able to control or change any tested yarn property. Some of the tests can be carried out by the spinner as an aid to consistent production, and again it is important that the spinner is adequately trained in the use of the test and understands the need to carry it out. Simple quality control, like simple testing, depends upon everyone concerned understanding the need for any change and being willing to modify existing practices to bring about an improvement in yarn quality.

Testing with greater accuracy

Measuring the properties of any textile yarn accurately requires both a wide range of testing equipment and considerable knowledge and experience of its use. If, for any reason, accurate testing is required it is normally best to send samples to a fully equipped and well established textile testing laboratory.

It is probably unlikely that, where yarn is being made on simple hand-operated spinning frames, very accurate testing will be required or indeed be necessary. All that is normally needed is to know if the yarn being made is too thick or thin, and if it has too much or too little twist, and to be able to change these properties in the desired direction. However, measurements to a greater degree of accuracy then the simple ones described so far will sometimes be useful, even if only as a quality control method. When testing the properties of any textile yarn the following points are important:

(a) All yarns, even with very good control of the spinning process, are extremely variable in all their properties. Testing any of these properties, therefore, requires that a representative sample of yarn is selected for testing, since the value of any measured property will be the average of a large number of tests.

(b) The properties of all textile fibres, and therefore the yarns made from them, vary according to the amount of moisture they contain. The most obvious example is weight. All fibres vary in the amount of moisture which they can naturally hold: wool for example can hold up to 30 per cent of its dry weight as water without feeling wet. Other fibre properties are also affected. The amount of moisture in a fibre is determined to a large extent by the temperature and humidity of the atmosphere. For this reason, a 'standard atmosphere' has been chosen for all textile testing. In temperate countries this is a temperature of 20° Centigrade (60° Fahrenheit) with relative humidity of 65 per cent, in tropical countries a temperature of 27° Centigrade (81° Fahrenheit), relative humidity 65 per cent. Since any variation in humidity and temperature brings about a change in properties, the results of any testing will not be comparable unless tests are carried out in the 'standard' conditions. If the testing room is not air conditioned with a controlled standard atmosphere, it is possible to use a small 'conditioning' cabinet which is maintained at the correct testing conditions and in which all yarns are placed for several hours before testing. The alternative is to make various allowances for any variation in atmospheric conditions, but this is not as satisfactory as testing properly 'conditioned' yarns. For many purposes, such as routine quality control tests, conditioning can be omitted provided that the atmospheric conditions do not vary widely from day to day.

Testing yarn counts

The most useful test which is likely to be needed is the count or yarn number and this can be obtained with relatively simple and inexpensive equipment.

The count of a yarn is a number which expresses its fineness. Since yarn thickness is variable and has only an approximate relationship to the count, the count is defined as the weight per unit length (direct yarn count systems), or the length per unit weight (indirect yarn count systems). Thus, to measure the count of a yarn it is necessary to measure an accurate length and weigh it.

Unfortunately many yarn count systems have come into use over the years, all using different units of length and weight: in this manual all counts are given in the Tex system which is being used more and more as a universal system. A chart is given in Appendix 3 showing how Tex compares to three other count systems.

In the Tex system, the unit of length is 1000 metres and the weight is in grams. Thus if 1000 metres of yarn weighs 30 grams, the yarn is 30 Tex.

The equipment needed is a hand-operated wrap reel with a circumference of exactly one metre and a weighing scale capable of weighing to an accuracy of 0.05 grams. The method is to select randomly 20 samples of the yarn to be tested and reel one 50-metre hank from each sample. The total weight of all the hanks (1000 metres) in grams is the count of the yarn in Tex. The hanks should if possible be conditioned in a standard atmosphere for at least three hours before weighing.

Testing amount of twist

The amount of twist in a yarn is another important property of spun yarns. The average twist inserted in a yarn is probably best estimated from the spinning frame settings, that is, by dividing the total revolutions of the spindle in a given time by the length of yarn produced in that time. This can be calculated by dividing the spindle speed, in revolutions per minute, by the speed of yarn delivery from the front draw rollers, in inches per minute. This will give the average number of turns per inch in the yarn. This is a more reliable method of estimating the average twist than by the use of a twist tester. However, it is sometimes useful to be able to measure twist, perhaps because the spinning frame settings are not available, or when looking for twist variations in a length of yarn. In these cases a twist tester must be used.

Measurement of twist with a twist tester

The most useful piece of equipment is probably a standard twist tester. This is a simple instrument which allows a length of yarn to be clamped between two sets of jaws. The jaws can be placed at varying distances apart, normally 1" to 10". One set of jaws rotates and is attached to a counter. The jaws are rotated and the number of turns needed to completely untwist the yarn noted. The number of turns divided by the length of yarn in inches will give the T.P.I.

The yarn to be tested must be sampled carefully, a minimum of 50 tests should be made for each yarn, measurements should be made at one-metre intervals along the yarn.

Although this instrument seems simple to use, care and practice are needed to achieve consistent results. Other yarn properties which are normally tested, such as strength and extensibility, evenness of all properties, really need a wide range of testing equipment and are outside the scope of this handbook.

If used consistently and sensibly, the simple tests described in this chapter will allow a small scale spinning operation to make yarn which has reasonably regular properties and which conforms to a specification. It cannot be overstressed that all testing must have a practical purpose and be a part of the production process. There must always be the intention to use the results of testing to control the production of what is being tested. It is thus of great importance to be able to control any property being tested. If control is poor or non-existent, there is absolutely no point in testing that particular property, other than by the most subjective methods.

4. SPECIFICATIONS OF SMALL-SCALE SPINNING MACHINES

This chapter is intended to be a survey of some small scale spinning machines that are currently available. Without attempting to be comprehensive, it describes a range which may be of interest in situations where new spinning activities are being started or existing activities extended. Drop spindles and spinning wheels are not included since they have been described in Chapter 2. Spinning wheel manufacturers are of course included in Chapter 6. Specifications are as accurate as possible, but obviously the output of any hand-operated machinery will vary very widely, being dependent upon many factors, from the quality of the raw material being spun, to the energy of the spinner.

MACHINE SPECIFICATION 1

Centrifugal pot spinner

These are one and two pot centrifugal spinners for hand operation. They can spin directly from card sliver which is fed to a four roller drafting system. After drafting the yarn passes through guides to the spinning pots which are driven by tapes or strings at up to approximately 20,000 RPM. The pots require a small addition of water during spinning to help in the formation of the yarn package. The output per pot is almost three times that of a hand operated ring spindle, but only relatively coarse yarns can be spun. Since the spinning pot is fixed to the machine the yarn must be removed from the pot by a separate operation.

Technical specification	*One pot*	*Two pot*
NO. OF POTS	One	Two
FIBRES	Cotton and blends	Cotton and blends
STAPLE LENGTH	14 to 19mm	14 to 19mm
COUNT RANGE	50 to 85 Tex.	50 x 85 Tex.
DRAFT RANGE	40	40
TWIST RANGE	15 TO 20 T.P.I.	15 to 20 T.P.I.
SLIVER RANGE	2000 to 3000 Tex.	2000 to 3000 Tex.
OPERATION	Hand	Hand
OUTPUT	400 to 700 gm/8hrs	700 to 1300 gm/8hrs

MACHINE SPECIFICATION 2

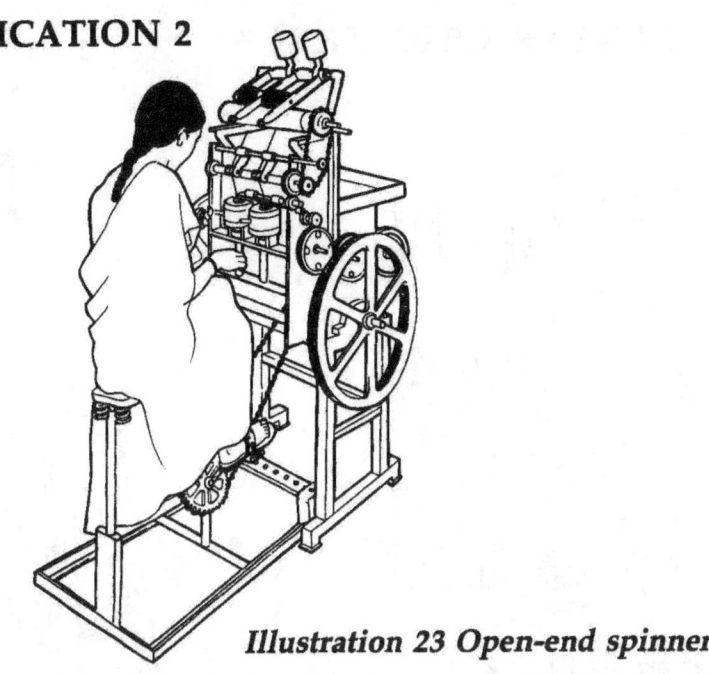

Illustration 23 Open-end spinner.

These are two- and four rotor open-end spinners. The two-rotor is for foot pedal operation, and the four-rotor for power operation. All machines can spin directly from carded sliver which is drafted in the two-rotor machine by a 4 roller drafting system and in the four-rotor machines by a combing roller. Only coarse counts can be spun but even the foot-powered machine has an output per rotor which is twice that of a hand-operated ring spindle. The two-rotor machine can be supplied with two additional rotors and power operation, output per rotor is higher and counts range extended. The other four-rotor machine is based upon standard components from large commercial machines but will operate from a domestic power socket.

Technical specification

No. OF ROTORS	2	4
FIBRES	Cotton and blends	Cotton and blends
STAPLE LENGTH	26 to 60mm	Up to 60mm
COUNT RANGE	100 to 300 Tex.	20 to 200 Tex.
DRAFT RANGE	11 to 36	25 to 200
TWIST RANGE	8 to 16 T.P.I.	5 to 50 T.P.I.
SLIVER RANGE	2000 to 5000 Tex.	2000 to 5000 Tex.
OPERATION	Foot pedal.	Power 1hp. motor single phase.
OUTPUT	800 to 3000 gm of 100 Tex yarn/8 hr	6000 to 8000 gm of 33 Tex yarn/8 hrs

MACHINE SPECIFICATION 3

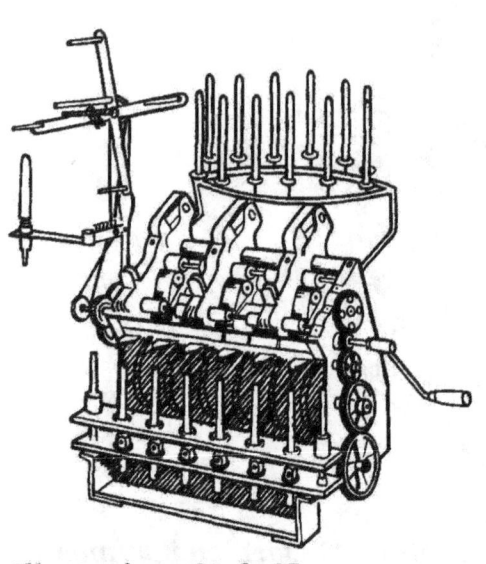

Illustrations 24 & 25
Ring spinning frames (charkhas)

These are all single sided ring frames (charkhas) for either hand or foot treadle operation. Machines with six to twelve spindles are available for spinning short staple fibres and four spindle frames are available for long staple fibres. Rovings are fed to a three roller apron drafting system with top arm weighing. After drafting the yarn passes through guides and is wound on to bobbin tubes. The spindles are driven by ropes from pulleys. Routine settings on the frame are simple and no adjustments are needed unless radical changes are made in the raw material being spun. Yarn count range can be changed easily through minor adjustments. Specifications for six, eight and twelve spindle charkhas are given.

Technical specification

No. OF SPINDLES	6	8	12
FIBRES	Cotton/blends	Cotton/blends	Cotton/blends
STAPLE LENGTH	21 to 38mm	20 to 40mm	20 to 40mm
COUNT RANGE	6 to 30 Tex	10 to 40 Tex	12 to 40 Tex.
DRAFT RANGE	17 to 20	17 to 20	17 to 20
TWIST RANGE	20 to 33 TPI	20 to 33 TPI	20 to 33 TPI.
ROVING RANGE	150 to 600 Tex	150 to 600 Tex	150 to 600 Tex
OPERATION	Hand	Hand	Foot treadle
OUTPUT	320 to 600 gm/8 hrs.	420 to 700 gm/8 hrs.	500 to 1000 gm/8 hrs.

MACHINE SPECIFICATION 4

Power-driven ring spinning frames

These are twenty- and twenty-four-spindle frames. The twenty-spindle is a shortened full size machine and the twenty-four-spindle is two, twelve-spindle hand-operated frames modified for power operation. Rovings are fed to three-roller apron drafting systems with either top arm weighing or hook and press weighting. The drafting system allows all staple fibres of up to 64mm length to be spun at drafts of up to 25, after drafting the yarn passes through guides and is wound onto bobbin tubes in the normal manner. Routine settings on the frame are straightforward and changes in count range require only minor adjustments.

Technical specification

No. OF SPINDLES	20	24
FIBRES	Cotton and blends	Cotton and blends
STAPLE LENGTH	UP TO 64 mm	Up to 64 mm
COUNT RANGE	10 to 50 Tex	10 to 50 Tex
DRAFT RANGE	Up to 25	10 to 20
TWIST RANGE	Up to 30 T.P.I.	20 to 30 T.P.I.
ROVING RANGE	150 to 600 Tex	150 to 600 tex
OPERATION	Power 1hp single phase	Power 0.75 hp single phase
OUTPUT	3000 to 4000 gm 30 Tex yarn/8hrs	3500 gm 25 Tex yarn/8hrs

5. PLANNING FOR PRODUCTION

The situations in which yarns are made on simple equipment are likely to vary widely. It may be intended to establish yarn production in a new situation, where there is little local experience and knowledge of spinning, or perhaps a well established local activity is to be improved or expanded. Whatever the intention, careful planning is important and a few basic requirements must be met to achieve successful production.

If spinning is to be organized in a centralized manner, rather than in individual households, the decision to do so must be made based upon the type and quantity of yarn needed to meet a particular known requirement. A supply of raw materials for spinning, in an appropriate form and in sufficient quantity, must be available on a regular basis. If raw materials have to be supplied from a distance the availability and cost of transport must be carefully assessed.

The way in which the spinning will be organized locally needs to be considered. The space or building in which it will take place can be arranged in any way which is most convenient but it should be dry, light and airy, with good shade. Spinning and storage of yarns or raw materials should never be in direct sunlight. The space should be arranged so that materials can be moved easily. The building should include a secure area to store both raw materials for spinning and yarns after spinning. The storage area should be light and have good ventilation. Raw materials such as rovings, and also finished yarns, should be stored off the ground on wooden shelves or slats, and in a way that allows frequent inspection for signs of attack by insects or mildew. All natural textile fibres are subject to such attacks and, in the absence of chemical treatment to prevent them, frequent inspection and turning, combined with storage in light and airy conditions out of direct sunlight are the best precautions.

It is unlikely that the spinning area will be air conditioned, so that ideal atmospheric conditions will not always be available. For most spinning 50-65 per cent relative humidity at 20-25°C will be reasonable. Very low humidity will cause most problems during spinning and if the atmosphere is very dry some water should always be present in the spinning area: perhaps some areas of the floor can be sprinkled or buckets of water left in several places. High humidity and temperature are an aid to spinning, but then there may be problems with mildew attack on any stored materials.

Some waste will occur during spinning from broken yarns and ends of rovings; these have some value and should be carefully collected and stored for sale as spinning waste.

The area in which the raw materials for spinning, such as rovings or slivers, are received should contain a bench and suitable weighing equipment to check on deliveries. It would also be useful to have a small area in which simple yarn testing could take place. Checking the count of the yarn being spun would be a useful quality control procedure.

If spinning is being introduced as a new activity to an area, or if a new type of spinning equipment is being recommended, suitable training should be considered an essential first step before production. Even with hand or power-operated spinning frames, skill and knowledge of the process will bring dividends in terms of yarn quality. If possible some training should be started, even if only for one or two key personnel, before the establishment of a new spinning unit. The training programme should also include discussions with all those who might be involved with the new activity. The social problems which may arise from a failure to introduce new ideas successfully and with local agreement, can be a major barrier to any new venture. Suitable training is sometimes available at major textile centres or educational institutions in the area and these possibilities should be investigated. Any training programme must also include the safety aspects of using new and perhaps unfamiliar equipment.

Before making any decisions about the scale of equipment needed in a new situation, or before modifying the existing type of equipment, the following points should be carefully considered.

COST Is there sufficient justification or need for the level of expenditure planned? Is there sufficient cash available to meet purchase costs? If money is borrowed for purchases, can it be repaid satisfactorily? Are there any local or government supported loan schemes to cover the capital cost of equipment or for the establishment of small industries? Is sufficient cash available to meet day-to-day running expenses, wages, work in progress, stocks?

CAPACITY Does the choice of spinning equipment match the desired yarn production and the availability of raw or processed material for spinning? Is there room for expansion? Is the spinning equipment flexible enough to give some variation in yarn types?

LOCATION If the spinning equipment and other facilities are located in one place, will this suit all those who expect to use it? Would temporary locations and portable equipment be more suitable? If materials have to be moved between different locations, is suitable transport available at reasonable cost?

AVAILABILITY Is the equipment available locally from a reputable manufacturer? If not, is anyone willing to manufacture or sell the equipment in the district? Are manufacturing instructions available and are there sufficient skills to carry out construction? What kind of spare parts and advisory service is on hand or will be needed? If power-driven equipment is being planned, is a reliable power supply available for a reasonable period each day?

EXPERIENCE Is the equipment easy to use? Can tuition be obtained locally or at a national training centre? What local skills exist, or could be trained, for maintaining and servicing the equipment?

SOCIAL ACCEPTABILITY Will the choice of equipment and system be readily acceptable to local people? What changes to existing social practice will be required? Has the demand for change come from the local community or from outside? After shortlisting the most suitable range of equipment, an economic evaluation of all inputs and outgoings associated with it will help to identify the best final choice. Finally, seek expert advice about the equipment and how you propose to use it before purchase.

Economics of yarn production
Once a spinning operation has been planned in some detail, it is a useful exercise to undertake a trial costing for the production of yarn to give a rough idea of the viability of the operation in commercial terms. The cost of any yarn has two components, overheads (fixed or indirect costs) and variable (direct costs).

Indirect costs

1. Interest on the cost of any stock of raw materials.
2. Cost of premises.
3. Heat/light/power.
4. Telephone.
5. Cost of depreciation on equipment and interest on any loans for purchase.
6. Consumable materials.
7. Insurance.
8. Postage/stationery.

Direct costs

1. Raw materials (rovings/slivers).
2. Wastage (10% for hand-spun yarn).
3. Transport costs.
4. Wages (including any contribution to a welfare fund and any incentive wages).

Once an estimate of production has been made for the planned spinning unit, the above costs can be worked out for, say, a week's production. The actual yarn costs are then the weekly indirect costs plus the weekly direct costs, divided by the number of units of yarn made per week. To this actual cost must be added any profit per unit of yarn to give the final selling price.

Useful information
The following information is given as a guide to planning only; it is obviously only possible to give approximate figures for the output of hand-operated machinery.

The example shown below is for the production of 33 Tex cotton yarn. (Production will be less for finer counts and more for coarser.)

	Hour	*8 Hours*
Drop spindle	7 grm.	56 grm.
Spinning wheel	10-12 grm.	80 grm.
Flyer type	14 grm.	112 grm.
6-spindle ring frame	66 grm.	528 grm.
12-spindle ring frame	120 grm.	900 grm.
24-spindle ring frame (power)	276 grm.	3000 grm.
4-rotor open-end spinner (power)	800 grm.	6000 grm.

One hand-loom weaver requires 800-900 grams of 33 Tex yarn for weft per 8 hours.

One power-loom weaver requires 3 kg of 33 Tex yarn for weft per 8 hours. A simple plan is given (Illustration 26) for a spinning unit of sixteen six-spindle ring frames with raw material and yarn storage areas. This unit would have an output of 48 kg of 33 Tex yarn per week which would supply the yarn requirements of 8 to 10 hand loom weavers.

SMALL SPINNING UNIT MODEL

1. Store for slivers and rovings and spun yarns. Small section for waste. All stored on open or slatted shelving.
2. Spinning area - each spinner plus six spindle manual ring frame requires approximately 1.5 x 1.5 metres floor area.
3. Area to receive slivers and rovings and dispatch yarn. Weighing scales and bench.
4. Small area for testing.

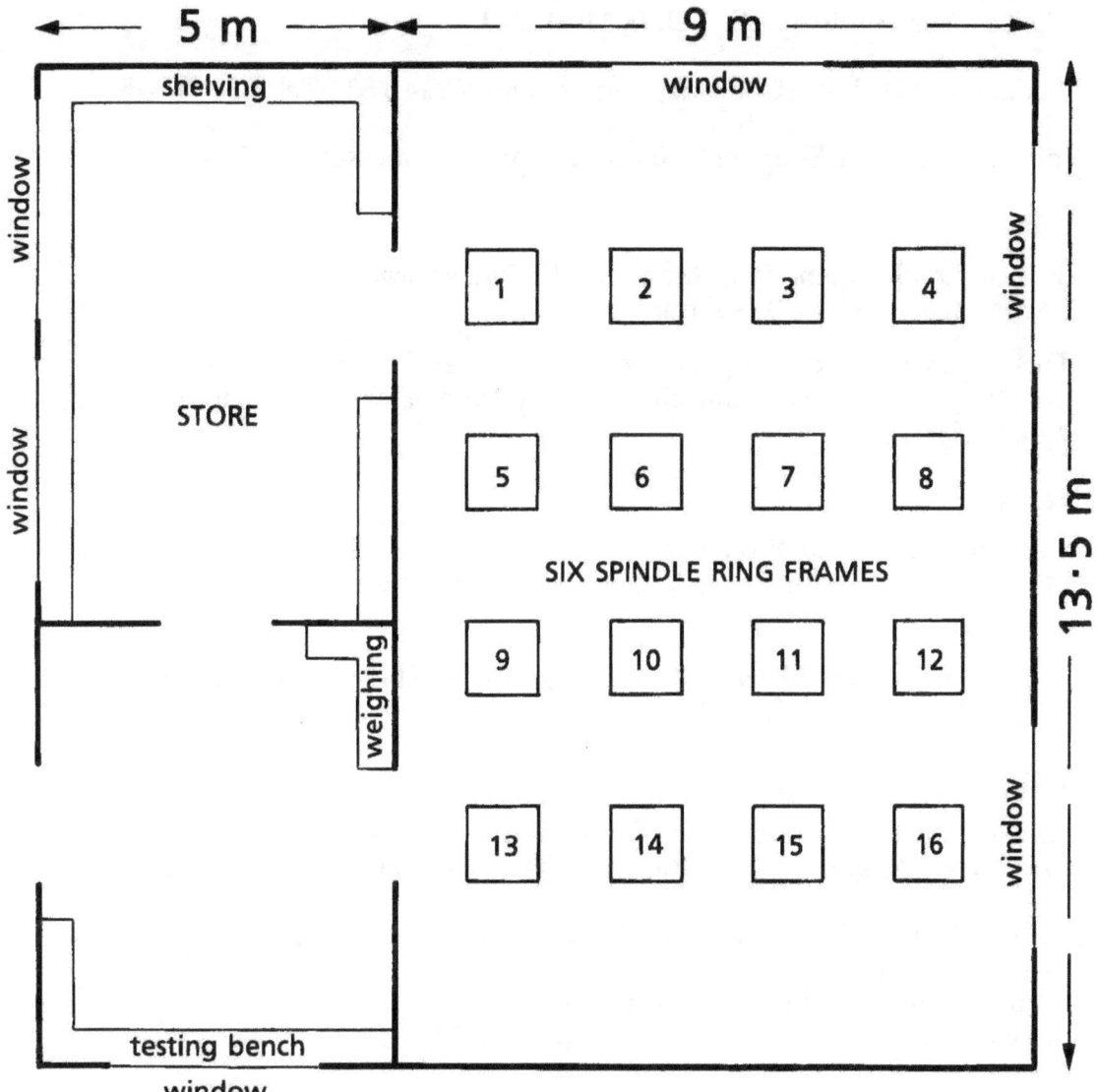

Illustration 26

6. EQUIPMENT SUPPLIERS

DROP SPINDLES AND SPINNING WHEELS

United Kingdom

Crowdy Wood Products Ltd., The Old Bakery, Clanfield, Oxford OX8 2SP.

Dingle Hill Products, J.A.N. Burra, Mid Gowden, Comrie, Tayside PH6 2HV.

Frank Herring & Sons, 27 High West Street, Dorchester, Dorset DT1 1UP. Tel. 0305 67917.

D.J. Williamson, 159 Main Street, Ashfordby, Melton Mowbray, Leicestershire LE14 3TS. Tel. 0644 812230.

Haldane & Co. Ltd., Gateside, Cupar, Fife KY14 7ST. Tel. 033 76 469.

Splinter Group, 1 Shepherds Barton, Frome, Somerset BA11 1EL.

India

Gujarat Khadi Gramodyog Mandal, Harijan Ashram, Ahmedabad 380 027, Gujarat.

(This organization can supply drop spindles and spinning wheels including 'Book or Box Charkhas' which are available in small or regular sizes.)

Nepal

Association for Craft Producers,
P.O. Box 3701, Kathmandu, Nepal. Tel. Kathmandu 2 16676

6, 8, 10, AND 12 SPINDLE RING SPINNING FRAMES FOR SHORT STAPLE FIBRES

India

Ambar Utpadan Vibhag, Sourashtra Rachnatmak Samiti, 20 Udyog Nagar, At P.O. Rajkot 360002. Gujarat.

Ambar Charkha Karyalaya, Tamilnadu Sarvodaya Sangh, At P.O. Veerapandy Tirrupur, 638605. Tamil Nadu.
Venue Scientific Industries, 146 Phase-1, Mayapuri Industrial Area. New Delhi 110064.

Sideco Equipment Complex, Kerala Small Industries Development
   Corporation, T.C. No. 24/1212, At Mettukada P.O. Thykand, Trivandrum
   695014, Kerala.

Shri Vaishnav Polytechnic, M.O.G. Lines,
   At P.O. Indore 452002, Madhya Pradesh.

Gujarat Khadi Gramodyog Mandal, Harijan Ashram,
Ahmedabad 380027, Gujarat.

Appropriate Technology Development Association,
   (A.T.D.A.), P.O. Box 311 Ghandi Bhawan, Lucknow 226001, Uttar
   Pradesh. Tel. Lucknow 33496.

4 SPINDLE RING SPINNING FRAMES FOR LONG STAPLE FIBRES

India

Gujarat Khadi Gramodyog Mandal, At Harijan Ashram,
   Ahmedabad 380027, Gujarat.

4 ROTOR OPEN-END SPINNER, POWER OPERATED

United Kingdom

Bradford University Research Ltd., University of Bradford,
   Great Horton Road, Bradford, W. Yorkshire BD7 1DP.
   Tel. 0274 733466 Telex 51309.

India

Iris Engineering Industries Ltd., Singanallur, Coimbatore 641005,
   Tamil Nadu, Tel. Coimbatore 87 546.

SINGLE- AND 2-ROTOR OPEN-END SPINNER, FOOT TREADLE OPERATED OR WITH POWER ASSISTANCE

India

Gujarat Khadi Mandal, Harijan Ashram, Ahmedabad 380027.

India

Iris Engineering Industries Ltd., Singanallur,
   Coimbatore 641005, Tamil Nadu, Tel. Coimbatore 87 546.

1- AND 2-POT CENTRIFUGAL SPINNERS, HAND OPERATED

India

Ambar Utpadan Vibhag, Sourashtra Rachnatmak Samiti,
 20 Udyog Nagar, At P.O. Rajkot 360002, Gujarat.

Ambar Charkha Karyalaya, Tamilnadu Sarvodaya Sangh,
 At P.O. Veerapandy, Tirrupur, 6838605, Tamil Nadu.

Venus Scientific Industries, 146 Phase-1,
 Mayapuri Industrial Area, New Delhi 110064.

Sideco Equipment Complex, Kerala Small Industries
 Development Corporation, T.C. No. 24/1212,
 At Mettukada P.O. Thykand, Trivandrum 695014, Kerala.

Shri Vaishnav Polytechnic, M.O.G. Lines,
 At P.O. Indore 452002, Madhya Pradesh.

Gujarat Khadi Gramodyog Mandal, Harijan Ashram,
 Ahmedabad 380027, Gujarat.

Appropriate Technology Development Association,
 (A.T.D.A.), P.O. Box 311 Ghandi Bhawan, Lucknow 226001,
 Uttar Pradesh. Tel. Lucknow 33496.

24- SPINDLE POWER OPERATED RING SPINNING FRAMES FOR SHORT STAPLE FIBRES

India

Appropriate Technology Development Association,
(A.T.D.A.) P.O. Box 311 Ghandi Bhawan, Lucknow 226001, Uttar Pradesh.
Tel. Lucknow 33496.

20- SPINDLE POWER OPERATED RING SPINNING FRAME FOR SHORT STAPLE FIBRES

India

Machine Products (India) Ltd, 696/7 Reid Road, Ahmedabad 380002, Gujarat.

Cassa Sales Pvt Ltd. Cassa chambers, Kagdapith,
 o/s Astodia Gate, Ahmedabad, 380022 Gujarat. Tel. 345678, 342345.

YARN-TESTING EQUIPMENT

United Kingdom

James Heal & Co. Ltd, Richmond Works, Lake View, Halifax, West Yorkshire HX3 6EP. Tel. 0422 66355 Telex 51450.

Shirley Developments Ltd., 856 Wilmslow Road, Didsbury, Manchester M20 8SA. Tel. 061 445 7757 Telex 669386.

WIRA Technology Group Ltd., Wira House, West Park Ring Road, Leeds LSl6 6QL. Tel. 0532 781281. Telex 557189.

Goodbrand-Jeffreys Ltd., Elm Works, Mere Lane, Rochdale, Greater Manchester OL11 3TE. Tel. 0706 32712. Telex 635300.

India

V.P.F. Testing Equipment, Venkatapathy Foundry, Peelamedu, Coiombatore 641004, Tamil Nadu.

M/S Kamal Metal Industries, Gajjar House, Astodia Road, Ahmedabad 380001, Gujarat.

7. SOURCES OF FURTHER INFORMATION

Most of the organizations mentioned below are useful sources of information. If detailed information is needed it is often important to know which department or individual to approach. ITDG in Rugby, U.K. is often able to give advice or direct enquiries to the appropriate person or department.

1. Research organizations. Many have information services which are available even to non-members.
2. Other useful sources of information including institutions, federations and guilds.
3. Written sources of information. This includes a selected list of publications used in the compilation of this manual.

(1) Research organizations

(a) They almost always have an information service on a wide range of textile topics. This usually includes book lists and copies of research papers.

(b) They will usually undertake testing or other work for which a charge is made.

(c) They sometimes organize courses or training programmes in aspects of textile manufacture.

United Kingdom

WIRA, Wira House, West Park Ring Road, Leeds LS16 6QL.
Tel. 0532 718381. Telex 557189.

International Wool Secretariat, Technical Centre, Valley Drive, Ilkley, LS29 8PB. Tel. 0943 601555. Telex 51457.

Shirley Institute, Didsbury, Manchester M20 8RX.
Tel. 061 445 8141. Telex 668417.

India

The South India Textile Research Association (SITRA), Coimbatore 641014, Tamil Nadu.

Ahmedabad Textile Industry Research Association (ATIRA), Polytechnic Post Office, Ahmedabad 380015, Gujarat.

Textile and Allied Research Association. (TAIRO),
Baroda, Gujarat.

Training courses in spinning can sometimes be organized at khadi centres by KVIC, Bombay, or directly at the Ghandi Ashram, KG Prayog Samsti, Ahmedabad 380027, Gujarat. Tel. 4)60524.

(2) Other useful sources of information

United Kingdom

The Textile Institute, 10 Blackfriars Street, Manchester M3 5DR.
Tel. 061 843 8457. Telex 668297.

The Crafts Council, 12 Waterloo Place, London SW17 4AU. Tel. 01 930 4811.

The Confederation of British Wool Textiles Ltd,
60 Toller Lane, Bradford BD8 9BZ. Tel. 0274 491241.

Knitting Industries Federation, 7 Gregory Boulevard, Nottingham NG7 6NB.

Association of Guilds of Weavers Spinners and Dyers, BCM 963 London, WC1N 3XX.

India

Khadi and Village Industries Commission, Irla, Vile Parle, Bombay 400056.

Centre for Appropriate Technology, Indian Institute of Technology, Hauz Khas, New Delhi. 110016.

Rajasthan Small Industries Corp. (RAJSICO),
2nd Floor, Udyog Bhawan, Tilak Marg, Jaipur, 302005.

Aga Khan Rural Support Programme, Choice Premises,
Swastik Crossroads, Navrangpura, Ahmedabad 380009, Gujarat.

(3) Published sources of information

Books about textiles which contain information on spinning (some of these can only be obtained from libraries*).

Hall, A.J., *Standard Handbook of Textiles* (Butterworth & Co.)

* Norton, W.E., & Wray, G.R., *An Introduction to the Study of Spinning* (Wira Library).

* Crockett, C., *The Complete Spinning Book* (Textile Institute).

* Fannin, A., *Handspinning* (New York, Van Nostrand Reinhold).

Baines, P., *Spinning Wheels, Spinners and Spinning* (Batsford Press).

Teal, P., *Hand Woolcombing and Spinning* (Blandford Press).

* Shaw, C., & Eckersly, F., *Cotton* (Pitman & Sons).

Brearley, A., *The Woollen Industry* (Pitman & Sons).

Atkinson, R.R., *Jute* (Temple Press).

Books and papers containing more specialized information on spinning.

De Barr, A.E., & Catling, H., *Manual of Cotton Spinning, vol.5* (Textile Institute).

* von Bergen, W., *Wool Handbook, vol.2, pt.1* (John Wiley & Sons, New York).

* Merrill, G.R., *Cotton Ring Spinning* (Lowell, Mass.).

WIRA, *Drawing and Spinning* (Wool Research, vol.6).

Shirley Institute, *Break Spinning*.

Dyson, E., Iredale, J.A., Parkin, W., *Yarn Production and Properties* (Textile Institute).

Nield, R., *Open-end Spinning* (Textile Institute).

* Paul, S.K., *Study in Modern Jute Technology* (Dasgupta & Co, Calcutta).

The Lodz Textile Seminars, no.3, vol.2, *Spinning* (UN, Geneva).

Wool Science Review, vol.14, 15, 16 (International Wool Secretariat)

Books on textile testing.

Methods of Test for Textiles (British Standards Institution).

Booth, J.E., *Principles of Textile Testing* (National Trade Press).

Norms for Spinning (SITRA).

Development and Transfer of Technology Series, No.4 (UNIDO, Vienna).

APPENDIX 1:
COMPARISON OF TEX WITH OTHER COUNT SYSTEMS

English cotton count and Tex

COTTON	TEX	COTTON	TEX
1	590	32	18.4
2	296	34	17.4
3	196	36	16.4
4	148	38	15.6
5	118	40	14.8
6	98.4	42	14
7	84.4	44	13.4
8	73.8	46	12.8
9	65.6	48	12.4
10	59	50	11.8
11	53.6	52	11.4
12	49.2	56	10.6
14	42.2	60	9.8
16	37	64	9.2
18	32.8	68	8.6
20	29.6	72	8.2
22	26.8	76	7.7
24	24.6	80	7.4
26	22.8	86	6.8
28	21	92	6.4
30	19.6	100	5.9

Metric counts and Tex

METRIC	TEX	METRIC	TEX
2	500	60	16.7
4	250	64	15.6
6	167	68	14.7
8	125	72	13.9
10	100	76	13.1
12	83.3	80	12.5
14	71.4	90	11.1
16	62.5	100	10
18	55.6	110	9.1
20	50	120	8.3
24	41.7	130	7.7
28	35.7	140	7.1
32	31.3	150	6.7
36	27.8	160	6.3
40	25	170	5.9
44	22.7	180	5.6
48	20.8	190	5.3
52	19.2	200	5
56	17.9	210	4.8

Woollen counts (Y.S.W) and Tex

WOOLLEN	TEX	WOOLLEN	TEX
6	320	27	72
7	280	28	70
8	240	29	66
10	195	31	62
11	175	32	60
12	160	33	58
13	150	34	56
14	140	35	56
15	130	36	54
16	120	37	52
17	115	38	51
18	107	39	50
19	102	40	48
20	96	42	46
21	92	44	44
22	88	46	42
23	84	48	40
24	80	50	39
25	78	52	37
26	74	56	35

INDIRECT-FIXED WEIGHT SYSTEM

English cotton count = no. of 840-yard hanks per pound

Galashiels woollen count = no. of 300-yard hanks (cuts) per 24oz

Yorkshire skeins woollen count = no. of 4,256-yard hanks per lb

Worsted count = no. of 560-yard hanks per lb

Linen count = no. of 1,000-metre hanks per kg

DIRECT-FIXED LENGTH SYSTEM

Tex count = no. of grams per 1,000 metres

Jute count = no. of pounds per 14,400 yards

Denier count = no. of grams per 9,000 metres.

APPENDIX 2: NOMOGRAM FOR TWIST FACTOR
(TEX AND YORKSHIRE SKEINS WOOLLEN)

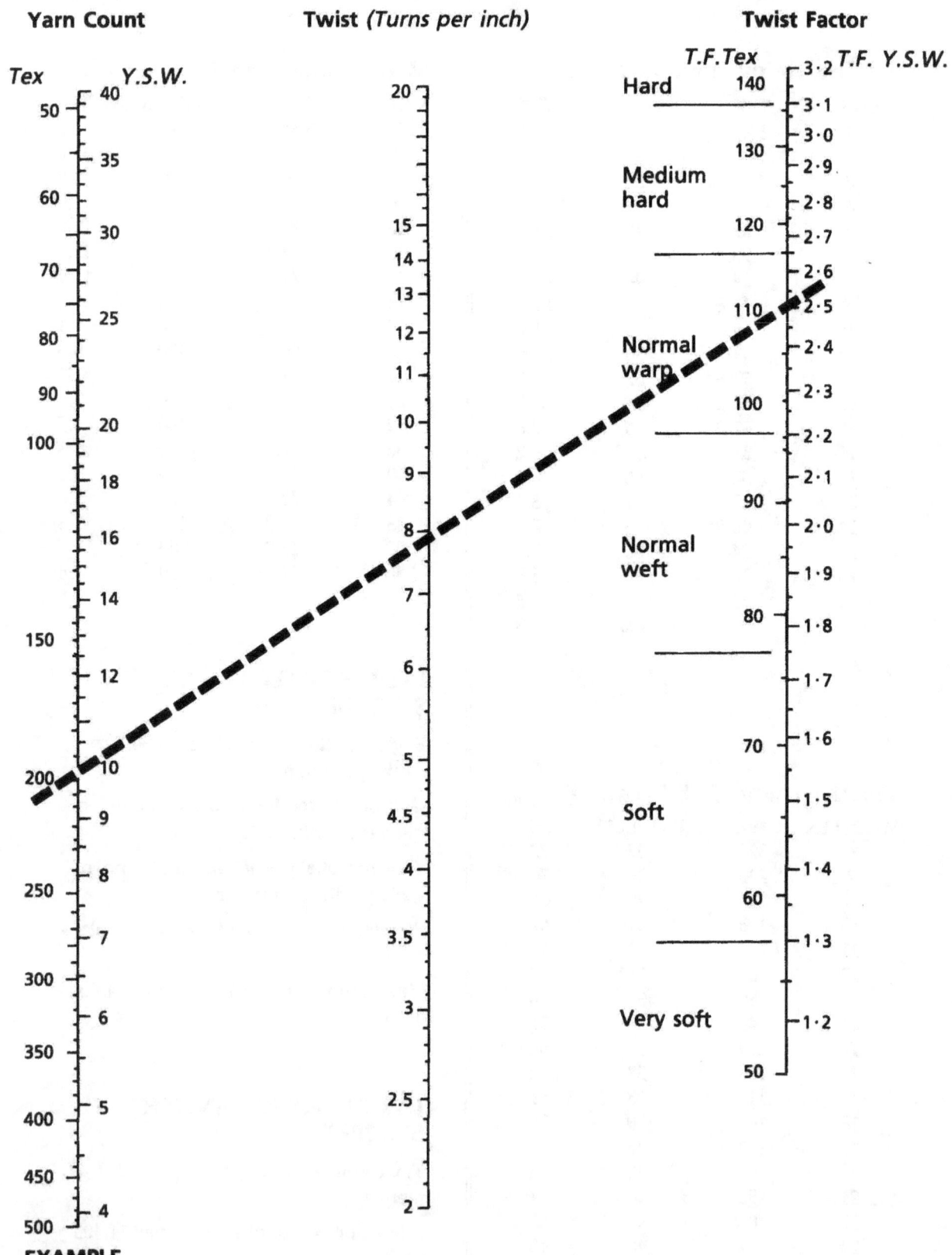

EXAMPLE

Question
What will the twist factor be when making a 10 Y.S.W. yarn with 8 T.P.I. (Turns per square inch) for normal warp

Answer
Diagram shows twist factor of 2.5

APPENDIX 3: NOMOGRAM FOR TWIST FACTOR
(TEX AND ENGLISH COTTON)

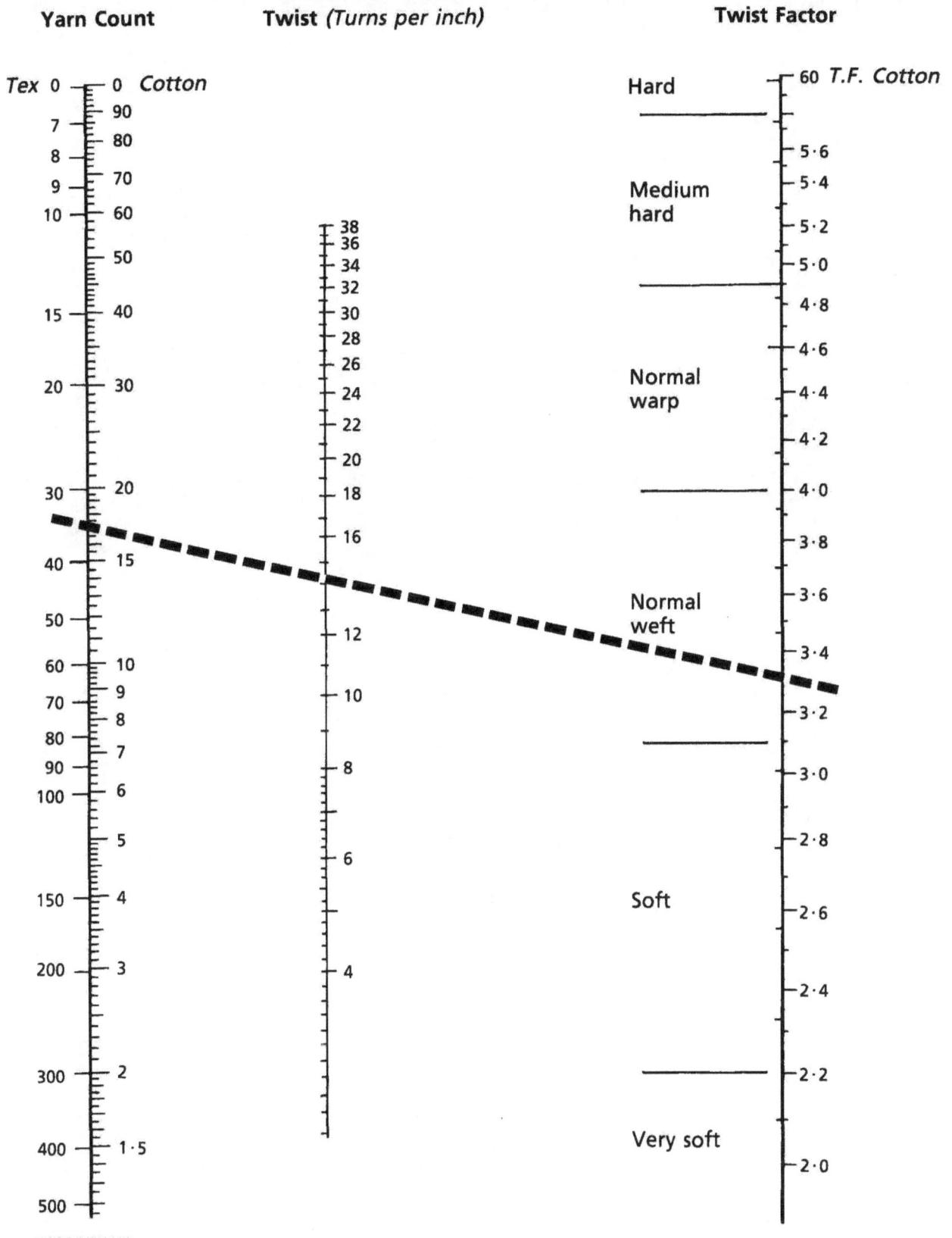

EXAMPLE

Question
How many T.P.I. (Turns per inch) would be needed to make a 34 Tex normal weft yarn (Twist factor 3.3)?

Answer
Diagram shows — 14. T.P.I.

www.ingramcontent.com/pod-product-compliance
Lightning Source LLC
Chambersburg PA
CBHW081237080526
44587CB00022B/3967